THE THOUGHTS OF
TRUEMAN NOW

THE THOUGHTS OF
TRUEMAN NOW
EVERY CRICKET MAN IAC'S ANTHOLOGY

Thoughts by Fred Trueman
Comments by Eric Morecambe
Illustrations by William Rushton
Compiled and edited by Fred Rumsey

Macdonald and Jane's London

© Fred Trueman 1978
© Illustrations William Rushton 1978
First published in 1978 by Macdonald and Jane's Ltd
Paulton House, 8 Shepherdess Walk, London N1 7LW
Second Impression 1978

ISBN 354 085220

Designed by David Fordham
Jacket photograph by Tony Evans

Filmset in Melior by
C. E. Dawkins (Typesetters) Ltd., London SE1, 1UN
Printed and bound in Great Britain by
Hazell Watson and Viney Ltd., Aylesbury, Bucks.

Contents

Foreword

As far as I am concerned Fred Trueman is one of the greatest fast bowlers that ever lived. He is the epitome of fast bowling. He has venom and charisma – that's the stuff you get on your shoulders. He has what all the commentators love – long hair. I think it was John Arlott who said that it looked like a lion's mane. He also had charisma from the back as he ran away from the camera. He inspired Tim Brooke-Taylor to write that wonderful radio programme, *Hello Cheeky*. He sent the ball down at 90-odd miles an hour and I was one of the people in the crowd who, if the batsman missed it, used to shout 'Oh! chicken, yellow, face up to him'. But to stand there in front of a ball coming down at that pace is no easy task. Eventually, towards the end of his career he was good with the bat. I feel that most bowlers want to be good with a bat. Augustine Snow, Dylan Willis and Leslie Underwood all want to go out and prove themselves with the bat rather than the ball. Ernie wants to be funny you know, poor sod.

Freddie has got everything going for him, he has stayed with cricket all the way through his life since he left the mines and started with Yorkshire. He made Yorkshire, he made England, and now he is making Trueman, which I think is important.

Freddie Trueman is still loved like Henry Cooper is. Henry never won a world boxing championship but he is more loved than any boxer in the history of boxing in this country.

Fred holds records – one was by Des O'Connor singing something or other, which I broke. Fred is what is known as the salt of the earth, you can't say fairer than that. If he was alive today I would tell him to his face.

E Morecambe

Introduction

On the following pages I have exposed my thoughts as I see cricket now in 1978. Some are old thoughts, some new, some you will agree with, some you will not, some you will find pompous, outrageous and unacceptable, a few you will find gentle, unassuming and benign. All add up to the way I feel about the game – in fact, thoughts of Trueman now. My old mate Eric Morecambe wanted his say, and his comments you will immediately recognise. Willie Rushton said he was an expert at graffiti, so it was either my lavatory wall or this book. First and nearest person to spell graffiti was Fred Rumsey who got the job of putting it all together. He said he owed it to me for taking my Test place. We are all united in our love for cricket and as Lord's Taverners put back into the game as much as we can. We hope you enjoy the book.

F Trueman

Editor's note
Although I can spell graffiti I don't know the first thing about publishing, so I am grateful to Rosalie Vicars-Harris for all her help and to David Fordham for his design. Peter Parfitt helped me with his thoughts and John Hughes with the facts. Christine Wood's typing was ten times quicker than mine.

Fred Rumsey

Bowling and all that

Bowling

I want to begin with fast bowling because that is usually how the game begins – as far as I am concerned.

A fast bowler must have a balanced run up. When I talk to youngsters to try and tell them about the run up, I ask them to think of a train leaving a station – how it sets off slowly and gathers momentum until it finally comes to its full speed. That is exactly what a bowler's run up is like. He sets off slowly with a short stride, gradually accelerating, and it's only in the last four yards up to the delivery stride that he should be travelling at his fastest pace. This really is where the pace of the ball comes from. The body is propelled forward with the front right arm coming round and pointing to somewhere near fine leg, if you are a right arm bowler, third man if you are left-handed. Your back arm at this point should be used somewhat like a ship's rudder. If you can run up to bowl and get yourself into a nice easy relaxed acceleration which has rhythm and balance you are at the beginning. As you reach your delivery stride with your left shoulder coming round, you are then looking over it straight down the wicket. This is the side-on position.

Willie, could you draw the side-on position?

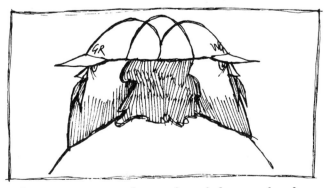

It upsets me to see the number of players who play square to the wicket, batting or bowling. Side-on cricket is not natural, it's not something you are born with, you have to learn it first. As you go into the body action, the arm (left arm if you are a right-hand bowler) starts coming over and this dictates the direction and the accuracy of the ball. If you can do all of that and follow through with the swing of the arm which propels the ball, the arm coming across the body and finishing outside the left knee, then you have a good bowling action. You stand a fair chance of swinging the ball. The next important thing to do is to make sure that you carry on in the follow through. Don't try to stop at the wicket because if you do you will have lost the acceleration that you have built up in your run up.

9

This is because you will try to stop too early. Finish seven or eight yards down the wicket. It is as important as the actual run up itself to keep the full flow of the bowling action and the bowling movement going. I swung the ball through the air and rarely did anything off the wicket. Others, more square on, did the reverse, particularly those with less pace.

To be a good bowler one has to be extremely fit. Now I remember Freddie Trueman in his early days. Freddie was so fit that he could actually jump six feet into the air — nine if you caught him right!

The quickest bowler I ever faced in any type of cricket was no doubt Frank Tyson. Typhoon they called him, which was a pretty good name. He was quicker than anything I had to face in my life. When he hit the bat you could feel it in the splice, he hit it so hard. I can tell you it was quite worrying when you looked behind and saw Keith Andrew and his slips vanishing up the pavilion steps just to get to their fielding position. The best fast bowler I ever saw was without doubt the great Ray Lindwall, he had a superb action, superb balance and rhythm in his run up. It has often been said that if Tchaikovsky had seen this man with his approach to the wicket,

AHA!
MY
NUT-CRACKER

the slow start, the beautiful acceleration coming in to the point of balance and delivery, he would have written a symphony to commemorate him. I think the best way to describe Ray would be a quick bowler who had a medium-paced bowler's accuracy,

with the ability to move the ball both ways. As a combination with Miller, they were deadly, as in fact are most good combinations. Quick bowlers like to hunt in pairs because they complement each other.

As a bowler I used to work on very simple principles, completely uncomplicated, which I have spoken to people about from time to time. I have seen them look at me with either amazement or disbelief or both. I don't know why but a mystique has grown up about bowling which really shouldn't be there. I always thought that I was lucky because I could field close to the wicket. So when Brian Statham or Frank Tyson or Peter Loader or Fred Rumsey was bowling at the other end, I would be fielding at either slip or leg slip and would be able to watch the batsman's first movement at close range, as the bowler delivered. This gave me, I always thought, a great advantage because being the same type of bowler, in the quick mould, by watching the batsman's first movement to these players, when they ran up to bowl I could tell what was happening when I bowled. Sometimes I noticed that he made his first movement when the bowler had three or four yards still to come. This is why, when I set off to bowl, the only thing I focused my eyes on was the batsman and his wickets because they were the two things I was after – to get the batsman out and to hit his wickets – certainly not the other way round. So with these thoughts in mind, the simple principles I worked on were as follows:

I studied the batsman and thought, he can play back, or he can play forward, he can play on the off-side, or he can play on the on-side – it was up to me to work out which was his preference. My approach was simple. If the batsman was a good back foot player I always used to pitch the ball that little bit further up, giving it a chance to swing that little bit later. If he was a front foot player then I knew that I would have to pull the ball down a little and bowl shorter because most likely he would be playing forward before I delivered. If he was a good off-side player, a strong off-side player, I would automatically bowl at his leg stump. If he was a good on-side player, I automatically bowled at his off-stump.

The speed of a fast bowler in his pomp has been measured on many occasions. Whether we could get a really true and accurate picture of how quick these men bowled I don't know. People talk about Harold Larwood bowling at 95 to 96 mph. This was taken by a man standing at the side of him half way down the wicket who pressed a stop watch as he started and delivered the ball and stopped it when the ball passed the wicket. I don't think this would really give a true indication, but at least we have some idea of a bowler's pace. Experiments of all

sorts have taken place and 90 mph seems to be the speed at which most fast bowlers bowl. The ball of course does not travel 22 yards as some people have suggested. It probably only travels 18. As it is very difficult to be able to get a true reading or a true timing of how fast a quick bowler can bowl, I don't really worry about it. What is more important to me is that fast bowlers are like jewels – when they appear everybody wants them. They are the players who win matches on all wickets, including the good ones.

Bowlers have always had a bit of banter with batsmen. Sometimes it gets out of hand and sometimes it's taken in good fun. I remember once bowling at some character from Gloucester who kept playing and missing and edging me through the slips. After he'd edged about four fours, I said to him, 'You've got more bloody edges on that bat than a cracked pee pot.' He said, 'I couldn't care less, I've paid for them, so I shall use the bloody lot.'

The only bouncers I know are in night clubs — there are two types. There are those that poke in your eye and the one who throws you out when you squeeze the others.

We hear many stories about the bouncer, particularly ones criticising its use. I maintain the bouncer is a legitimate part of the quick bowler's armoury. I must say here and now that whenever I hear bowlers say, 'I like to see blood on the wicket', or, 'I like to hit a batsman', I feel very sorry for them, because they must have something wrong with them, some kind of warped mind. I never went out with the intention of trying to hit people or cripple them. I used to bowl bouncers at people who couldn't hook, and at people who could hook. I used to bowl bouncers at people who couldn't duck and those who could duck, like Tom Graveney, Colin Cowdrey and Peter May. The people who ducked and got out of the way and let the ball go over the top, actually could laugh at you, because you were wasting your energy. The only advantage you gained by bowling a bouncer at these people was to sow the seeds of doubt in their minds that whatever your age or the state of the wicket, you could still bowl the bouncer. It is a very legitimate part of a fast bowler's armoury, but I hate to see it being abused as sometimes it is by certain bowlers in world class cricket today.

Bill Bowes, one of Yorkshire's great fast bowlers, very rarely batted. He had a hard time if he batted eight times in a year. He had a wonderful record that nobody else probably wants, and that is that he got a thousand wickets before he got a thousand runs. Bill had always enjoyed the luxury of bowling bouncers at tail-enders and never had to take it back himself because he so rarely batted. One day Yorkshire ran into trouble against Northamptonshire and Bill had to go in at number eleven. Nobby Clark, the tall left-arm fast bowler who played for England, was rolling his sleeves up even further than normal. As Bill walked in Nobby said, 'I've waited ten years for this moment', and he let go two or three bouncers at Bill right, left and centre. Anyway Bill, not to be outdone, had Northampton in trouble. He'd got six or seven wickets and the great Hedley Verity bowling at the other end got a wicket, and in came number eleven, Nobby Clark. As Nobby approached the wicket, Bill watched him all the way with a look that said, I've got you now. Hedley Verity ran up to bowl the first ball. Nobby Clark dashed down the wicket and missed it by a mile. Arthur Wood, the wicket keeper, took the ball and was holding it over the top of the stumps. Nobby turned round and said, 'You can take the bastards off Arthur, because I aren't coming back.'

The fast bowler was wrapping the bouncers around a batsman's earholes, he was ducking and diving, cursing and swearing, and after about four or five overs he turned to the bowler and said, 'There's one thing for certain, I've weighed you up.' 'What's that?' said the bowler. 'You'll never suffer from meningitis.' 'Why's that?' said the bowler. 'Because it's a bloody brain disease', said the batsman.

As a quick bowler I hated to see people batting in glasses. I always thought it very dangerous because they could play forward and the ball might bounce, get a top edge and smash their glasses into their face. On many occasions I used to think I daren't bowl a bouncer at this fellow, in case I hit him. I must admit I have hit people who wear glasses because I only used to *think* about not doing it. Fortunately the glass has never gone into their eyes because, due to modern scientific techniques, we now have a kind of perspex that doesn't shatter. Geoff Boycott and Mike Smith have played in them

more time to get into position against the medium-fast bowler than they do against the fast bowler. His ingredients, like run up, action, sideways-on at the bowling crease are similar to that of the fast bowler, although there is a tendency for more square on bowlers in this category. The length is different, he can't bowl as short as a fast bowler. He's got to bowl that little bit further up or he will be cut and pulled. There are two distinct types of medium-fast – and medium bowlers – the ones who swing the ball and the ones who rely on seam and movement off the wicket. The actions of fast medium-paced bowlers tend to vary a lot. They also bowl off a braced front leg which pivots on the crease. This is unlike the genuine fast bowler who tends to bowl through his front leg with his toe pointing towards the batsman.

To decide who was the best medium-paced bowler I ever ran up against is easy. In fact, I played my first Test match with him against Australia in 1953. It is, of course, Alec Bedser of Surrey and England, known as big Al. In 51 Test matches this man took 236 wickets on all types of tracks. He was something a little extraordinary, because he bowled with a sideways-on action but bowled big inswingers and he made the ball go very late. He was an intelligent bowler who could bowl to his field, and like all great bowlers he had that little something up his sleeve. Alec Bedser could bowl a deadly leg cutter. He called it a leg cutter but the way he held it in those massive hands,

for ages. I am very glad that contact lenses have been invented. It has taken a lot of fear out of the fast bowler's mind, fear that they might hit someone and blind them.

 *It must be very difficult for batsmen who wear glasses to bat because of the danger element. I know if I was asked to play for England, and, as you know I wear glasses, the first thing I would do would be to raise them. I would then be out first ball, because without my glasses I can't even hear.*

Medium-fast bowling differs from that of real quick bowling because the medium-fast bowler has to be far more accurate than the fast bowler. The fast bowler can get away with bad deliveries because of his pace. A medium-paced bowler cannot. If he is not constant to line and length and movement of the ball, which are his main ingredients, he is going to give runs away. Batsmen have

I would have thought it was more a fast leg break. He could bowl it on crumbling dry wickets or he could bowl it on rain affected wet wickets, and on many occasions to great effect. He was probably the greatest exponent of the leg cutter that I ever saw, and with his medium-paced swing bowling, plus the way he moved the ball about off the seam, it made him the most effective bowler of his time.

There was a medium-paced bowler one day bowling at a batsman who was 130 not out. He had never played against him before and he suddenly stopped, took a long look and said, 'Good God'. 'What's the matter?' said the batsman. 'Has anyone ever told you that you are the ugliest man in the world, certainly the ugliest I have ever seen in my life? It puts me off my bowling.' The batsman said, 'Well I can't help that'. 'No', said the bowler, 'but you could have stayed at home'.

Chinaman and googly bowlers are left-hand bowlers bowling out of the back of the hand, like George Tribe, Jack Walsh and of course Johnnie Wardle. The funny thing is that they need the same type of wicket as the fast bowler, in other words – a hard one, where they can get the ball to bounce. When you are spinning the ball out of the back of the hand on slow turning wickets, the batsman can play for the spin or the turn by meeting it, or waiting for it. But there is no batsman in the world who

likes playing a bouncing ball. They don't know how high, or how low it is going to bounce. Batsmen would much rather play on a wicket that is taking a bit of spin where they can play bat and pad, than they would on a hard wicket where the ball is liable to bounce any height. The leg spinner and the Chinaman googly bowlers coming out of the back of the hand and over the top, do tend to make the ball bounce more than the more orthodox left-arm or right-arm, off-spin bowler. A slow bowler has a completely different attitude, a different mental set up from fast bowlers. There's no good fast bowler that hasn't got some fire in his belly. The slow bowler has to serve an apprenticeship. It is said that spin bowlers are better bowlers after they are 30 years old and from what I have seen in my career, I think that is a true statement. It is a trade that has to be learned the hard way and sometimes it can be very painful.

A lot of people know the different terms for bowling, like left-arm, slow or Chinaman. Now I could never bowl a Chinaman, but I had a very good ball of my own. It was called the German – when it came down you didn't know which way it was going, east or west.

MARTIN ABOUT TO DELIVER THE BALL.

MARTIN AFTER DELIVERY.

It is very hard for me to decide who is the best slow bowler I ever played with or against, because in my time there were four or five really good ones. Johnnie Wardle, the Yorkshire slow left-arm bowler was one of the best. He had an immaculate length, making the batsman play forward ball after ball, on all types of wickets. If we were playing on a good wicket it was great to be able to have two bowlers in one, because Johnnie Wardle could bowl the Chinaman and googly as well as his orthodox left-arm spin. I think he was one of the finest exponents of the 'out of the back of the hand' stuff, that I have ever seen. I remember once when against Australia, I think it was in 1956 at Bradford, we were trying to get the last two out and Johnnie was bowling at the tail end; I said to him, 'John, why don't you have a go with a Chinaman against the number eleven?'. He said, 'I haven't bowled it since last year'. I replied, 'Have a go anyway, we've only got about ten minutes'. He came up and pitched a perfect Chinaman on a perfect length about off stump. It turned, went through the gate and hit leg and middle. It was an absolutely superb exhibition of bowling from a man who hadn't bowled that type of delivery for probably nine months. He was that good. I would put him on a par with anybody in the world today.

Toey Tayfield of South Africa was one of the finest off-spin bowlers I think I ever saw.

Running close to him of course would be Jim Laker from Surrey. Richie Benaud, the leg spin bowler from Australia had a tremendous control, which is the most important ingredient for leg spin bowling. Lance Gibb of the West Indies must also come into the reckoning. Lance is a bowler who never leaves you alone. He turns very quickly at

Batting

Batsmen, like bowlers, come in all shapes and sizes – it is said that great batsmen are on the diminutive side, 5ft 5in. or 5ft 6in. Some say that players as tall as Tony Greig have an advantage because this makes the bowler try to bowl a different length – but really I don't know. Look at Wally Hammond, he was a rather big built, powerful looking man. Len Hutton and Don Bradman were only slight people. Colin Cowdrey was rather heavy as was Colin Milburn. Tom Graveney was tall and slim, Denis Compton was about 5ft 9in. – rather well built. Bill Edrich was on the small side. Cyril Washbrook, one of England's top openers since the war, was a fairly stocky type of fellow. Reg Simpson was a tall man. The smaller batsmen seem to be able to play quick bowling as well as anybody. I suppose that is because if you bowl a bouncer at a small man, he is in a pretty useful position. He's much lower to have a hook, or if he doesn't want a hook he hasn't got that far to duck, which a tall man has if he gets into trouble with a bouncer. It does create difficulties for the bowler sometimes when he has to alter his length, bowling to a tall man with a very small batsman at the other end. On the whole batsmen tend to be on the small side and slightly built. When you actually meet them, it is amazing to see the thinness of their arms. Which goes to prove that it must be the timing and coordination of eye, brain and limb, all working together, that provides powerful shots. Peter May would really belt the ball and it would go past you in the field like a rocket. On the other hand Colin Cowdrey just stroked it with perfect timing and you will be surprised to know that the ball would go past you at practically the same pace as Peter's, who appeared to hit it with everything he had got.

There are certain types of batsmen who can play both on the on- and off-side, and off the front foot or the back foot. These, of course, are the great players, Garfield Sobers, Len Hutton, the great Donald Bradman, Weekes, Worrell and Walcott. They are people who I would call super-stars. The modern ones that come into this type of category, and I would say there are only three, are Barry Richards of South Africa, Viv Richards of the West Indies and Greg Chappell of Australia. These were the type of batsmen that I really liked to bowl at because I felt that they would bring the best out of me. If you were six inches off line or six inches over length, they would take complete advantage of you. You may be surprised that being a Yorkshireman I have left Geoff Boycott out of the list, but Geoff Boycott is a different type of player, who plays a different role. Geoffrey Boycott's role is anchor man, at which he is superb. Geoffrey is the type of player who scores at his own pace through

domination of the crease, with the most immaculate defence, and is a very difficult man to get out of position. He is not the classical stroke playing entertainer, although in the end he is probably just as effective if not more so. Every side has to have an anchor man if they want a complete team. The anchor man for England before Geoff Boycott was Ken Barrington, who did it most successfully, particularly when he was surrounded with players like Peter May, Colin Cowdrey, Ted Dexter and Tom Graveney.

For me, opening the batting is the most difficult thing to do in cricket. To walk out and start playing hostile bowling is extremely hard. The first thing you have to have is a bat. If you haven't got a bat, you have no chance. If you have a bat you have a fair chance. Now England have had a lot of players in recent years who had no chance because they have walked out to the wicket without their bats, or at least it looked that way.

Left-handers sometimes worry bowlers because of the need to change the line. I think I was a very fortunate bowler here because against the right-handed batsman my line of attack was by bowling close to the wickets, pitching leg and middle. So, if a left-handed batsman came in to bat against me with a right-hander at the other end, I didn't have to change the line, I could still bowl to him off and middle which was my natural line anyway. So sometimes I think God smiled on me.

There are batsmen, of course, who play every stroke in the book – what is known as being able to play shots all round the wickets. These are usually nimble-footed batsmen who as soon as you bowl a bouncer at them, are in the right position to play the hook shot. What I do notice about a lot of people who hook the ball in today's cricket, is that they hook in the air, they don't hit it down. I think that good hookers are people who hit the ball down or hit it down in front of square. Anyone hitting the ball and getting caught at fine leg was obviously in a good position to hook, but not the perfect one. Instead of getting six and out, think of getting a hundred. The good hookers who could hit between

mid-wicket and in front of square were players like Peter Burge, Don Bradman, Denis Compton and Bill Edrich. It may surprise you to know that the great Len Hutton just didn't bother to hook at all. There is always a man who is opposite to what we think should be done because Tom Graveney of Gloucester and Worcester hooked the ball off the front foot which was really extraordinary. It means that even to the quickest bowlers he is playing the ball at least three feet earlier than the batsman who plays off the back foot. In fact thinking about it, Brian Close also played off the front foot. The great Herbert Sutcliffe always told me that you had to get inside the line of the ball to hook and if anyone bowled a bouncer outside the off-stump, he didn't attempt to have a go at it. I know that if I am bowling a bouncer to a compulsive hooker, the place I would bowl it is somewhere outside the off-stump, relying on the man's pride getting the better of him. By not ducking at Freddie Trueman he would have to hook the ball from outside the off-stump, and there is no way that he can keep it down. There is only one way it can go and that is up. So if you are attempting to bowl a bouncer at a man you know will have a go, bowl it outside the off-stump and give yourself a chance of having him caught behind or somewhere around fine leg.

 *The best hooker I ever met was a young girl who used to work in Soho. She had the best inside pull I have ever known. That's why I wear glasses and Geoff Boycott always wears contact lenses.*

IT'S NO PLACE FOR MISTLETOE EITHER

50 in county cricket that day. To watch him at close range was a real pleasure. His bat was as wide as a barn door. To try to get him out of position was the ultimate aim of any bowler, but to do it was almost impossible. Without exaggeration, I have seen him play the same ball back, forward, change his mind and play half way back and still middle the ball. He had the knack of being able to hit the ball early or late as the situation demanded. I've actually seen him drive to third man with a con-

trolled shot. To watch him at his best was to enliken him to a ballet dancer, he was so light on his feet. He had an accident during the war which left him with one arm 2 to $2\frac{1}{2}$in. shorter than the other. It was his left arm and that is the guiding master of most batsmen. I remember him once saying that his left arm ached a bit and that the bat was probably a little bit too heavy for him even though it only weighed about 2lb 2oz. I once saw him bat with a Harrow size, which is a youngster's bat, and make a hundred with it. That is how good he was. Some say I exaggerate when talking about Leonard, but believe me, I am not exaggerating when I say he was the greatest batsman I ever saw in my life. The time I batted with him at Bristol, I remember him saying to me, 'They are going to take the new ball and George Lambert and C. J. Scott are not the worst of bowlers, but don't worry I'll take them.' Which he did, and for eight overs I might just as well have been in the stand with the crowd, because I never faced the ball and never even looked like doing so. When he said, 'come one', off the last ball of every over, he placed it so beautifully we didn't have to run, we walked.

Last year Fred gave me a Christmas Box. It's exactly the same as a cricket box except it has holly in it. It's made me very religious – I now pray that no ball ever hits me there.

The best batsman I ever saw without question of doubt on all wickets, was Len Hutton. What a player this man was. The first time I ever had the pleasure of shaking hands with him was in 1949 during my first Roses match. The first time I had the pleasure of batting with him was at Bristol in 1954 when Yorkshire was in trouble. He hadn't been feeling very well and had dropped down the order to number six or seven. Anyway, I made my first

The night watchman is a position usually held by tail-enders and is usually applied at the end of the day. If there are ten minutes to go and a wicket falls the low end batsman who goes in is called the night watchman. He is there to protect his batsmen

from quick bowlers and fading light. Some have been known to take a single off the first ball of an over, but the majority seem to do their job correctly. Quite a few have proved very awkward the next day finishing up getting 60 or 70. It only happened to me once. I went in as night watchman at Perth in Australia and finished up the next day getting 50. Some go in and get bowled out first ball. I can't always see the sense in it except in the case where the night watchman is a number eight batsman and he has some idea about batting. So if he does happen to stay in and bat for an hour the next day, it would be worthwhile. He could take the shine off the new ball if there is one, and also help get rid of the quickest bowlers. Then when the batsmen appear they are not up against top class pace and

by the time the top class fast bowler gets on, they have got used to the pace of the wicket and the light. The Australians generally do not believe in a night watchman and always send in the next batsman.

I will say a little about the night watchman, because I only know little night watchmen, people like Derek Underwood, who have to go out late at night, early in the batting order when their position is usually ninth, tenth or eleventh. I have seen them come out many times and sit in that little hut giving cocoa and Ovaltine to everybody.

At one time tail-enders were known as cannon fodder especially in the old days when players and umpires used to have to try and get away from the ground early on the last day, because they were probably travelling 200 miles or so. In fact it has been said that tail-enders were given out lbw because the umpire had to travel home and they became known in the game as train decisions. I believe a tail-ender should try to learn to bat. There are days when it comes in handy, particularly when their side is in a bad position. If they are able to get their head down and stay with a good player, he will be able to get enough runs to give his side some sort of realistic score for the bowlers to bowl at.

FANCY GOING FOR A QUICK SINGLE?

There are still too many tail-enders in the game who think that their job is to bowl or keep wicket, and that batting is for the batsmen. They are not right. What they should do is think of the extra service they can give to their side by scoring 10 or 15 runs. By the same token it's no use being a batsman and believing that because you have scored 50 you can then give away 40 by bad fielding, because that brings your score down to 10 and if you get nought in the second innings and you field as badly again, you are minus 30 — not a good score. A cricketer must at all times try to look at things in a balanced way. If he can get 15 runs it might make up for a wicket he didn't take. If he can save 10 runs it makes his 50 into a 60. This is the type of attitude I think that players should take into the game, especially at first class level, which after all is their living.

Wicket Keeping

I would think the most demanding job of any person in the fielding side, must be that of the wicket keeper. Whether he is standing back or standing up he has to watch every delivery. He has to concentrate on every delivery and if he does not concentrate his wicket keeping standard will start to lessen. It does help, I have always thought, for a wicket keeper to be like an ideal scrum half in rugby union – a little on the small side with his backside close to the floor. He has to be extremely nimble-footed and very quick to pick up the line of the ball from a position outside the off-stump. It is much more dangerous than it appears at first sight, particularly when standing up and having to take the ball down the leg side. Apart from the ball there is the danger of the batsman hitting you when swinging. Wicket keeping is a specialised job, it is not a very easy position and is a very demanding one.

If I was keeping wicket I would fear the ball most of all, there is no argument about that. That ball coming down at a 150 mph if Freddie, Brian Statham or Denis Lilley were bowling – no not Freddie, 12 mph because he's gone you know. I would even be able to catch him. Nowadays when you face Freddie his stomach gets to you before the ball does.

The best wicket keeper, and there were many in my time, was Godfrey Evans. Jimmy Binks, Don Brennan, Keith Andrew, Arthur McIntyre, Alan Knott, John Waite from South Africa and Wally Grout of Australia all stood out from the pack. But above them all, for me, was Godfrey Evans of Kent

and England. What a character this man was. He kept everybody going on the worst days at home or abroad. He was a jovial sort of character always ready for a joke. He was a wit. Above all he was a most competent keeper. To see him standing up to Alec Bedser on a green wicket was absolutely fantastic. His taking of the ball down the leg side and stumping was something to be seen to be believed. I remember in that famous Test trial at Bradford in 1950, when Jim Laker took eight for two, Alec Bedser bowled me a late inswinger. It went between my bat and pad, down the leg side and Godfrey Evans stumped me. Certainly one of the finest pieces of wicket keeping I have ever experienced. Godfrey's famous words, which kept us all going when we were flagging, were, 'Well, we'll be there at the finish boys, it's drinks at 6.30 p.m.'

Only two great keepers come into my mind instantly, world class keepers, Godfrey Evans and Alan Knott and not necessarily in that order. The rest would have trouble keeping pubs.

All-Rounders

England were particularly unfortunate in never really having the complete cricketer. In my entire career I think I only saw one complete player who did everything – he fielded at short leg, he caught them at slip, he bowled left-arm over the wicket, medium-fast swung the ball very late, he bowled left-arm orthodox, he bowled left-arm googlies and Chinamen. He was a man who could win a game completely on his own, and that was the great Garfield Sobers. For me Garfield Sobers is the greatest cricketer that ever lived.

The best all-round cricketer was W. G. Grace. Now I never saw W. G. Grace play and I wouldn't have known he was the best all-round cricketer but Ernie happened to see him and told me.

I think the two most famous slow bowler/batsmen of my Test career to come out of England must have been Ray Illingworth and Freddy Titmus. I can't think of anyone else who would come into their category, both of them in their time doing the double in county cricket on more than one occasion.

The best medium-fast bowler/batsman that we had during my time was definitely Trevor Bailey, an all-rounder of class, who would always be in my side if I was picking one – the old barnacle himself, what a cricketer this man was. He was a man who never gave in and on more than one occasion has frustrated bowlers into an early retirement. He was a man who gave nothing away and expected nothing to be given.

There have been many fine fielder/batsmen. I think straight away of Colin Cowdrey who was a great slip fielder who stood at first slip and took some absolutely brilliant catches, and everybody,

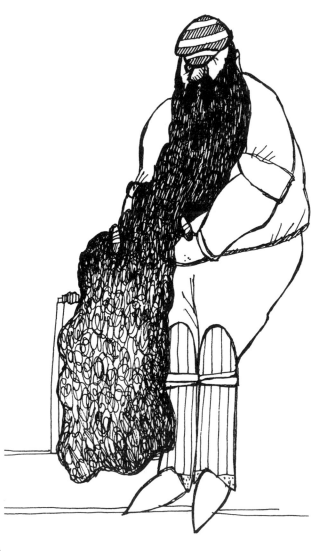

In England finding all-rounders of Test match standard has always been a very difficult thing to do. It always amazes me how easily Australia produces them. Among them are slow bowler batsmen like Richie Benaud, who was a superb all-rounder and Alan Davidson who was a quickish left-arm bowler, a wonderful bat and a brilliant fielder. There are also people like Ron Archer and Keith Miller. But in England for some unknown reason, we have really struggled at Test match level. We have always had players who are specialist quick bowlers or specialist spin bowlers, and if they could bat it was just a bonus.

of course, knows about his batting feats. Peter May was a useful close-to-the-wicket fielder and possibly, in my opinion the best young cricketer moulded into a top class batsman since the war. I think if an early retirement had not come along, he would certainly have been way past the 100 century mark. He was a great player. Ted Dexter was a very useful cover point fielder. Ken Barrington is another one who used to catch them at slip quite well, and we don't have to talk about his batting feats either, they will go on for ever. Tom Graveney, one of the most stylish batsmen of all time, was also another great slip fielder.

The best wicket keeper/batsman I ever played with of course, was the incomparable Godfrey Evans again. I saw him make a couple of Test centuries and he was a far better batsman than people ever gave him credit for. This was possibly because of his gay cavalier attitude to the game. But when the chips were down, he could get his head down and fight it out. So sure was he of his batting that one season he took a bet, which I think amounted to £100, that he would score 1500 runs if he could go in at number three or four. The bet was struck with his captain who pushed him up to number three and four and Godfrey, determined as ever, went on and scored 1500 runs in that season, just to win the bet. You can't get over the confidence of the man, he absolutely bubbled with it. When he really got cracking with the bat, he was a very quick scorer indeed, somebody who believed in hitting the ball. He also believed that his wicket keeping wasn't enough contribution towards his side that he must be included also for his batting, which I think he proved to very great effect.

The best wicket keeper/batsman in recent seasons has no doubt been Alan Knott, the England wicket keeper, who for me is a top class player whatever he is doing. He could have held his own with batting never mind his wicket keeping. After all he is the only wicket keeper to score over 4000 runs in Test cricket. Some specialist batsmen would be very pleased to have got 4000 runs without having to keep wicket. Another wicket keeper batsman Jim Parks actually played in four Test matches as a batsman, before he was selected by England to keep wicket.

Arthur Wood, that great character, was playing in a Test match against Australia and batting quite low down. England had scored over 700 runs and he had to go in and bat. He made 50 odd and when he returned to the pavilion a patron said, 'Well batted indeed Wood'. He replied, 'Thank you, I always was the man for a crisis.'

It has been said in cricket, beer is for bowlers, women are for batsmen, and God bless the all-rounders.

Fielders

I have had to think very carefully about my best fielder because there are so many different positions. I would say that the five best cover-point fielders I've seen were Neil Harvey, Norman O'Neill of Australia, Clive Lloyd of the West Indies, Colin Bland of South Africa and Ken Taylor of Yorkshire and England. The finest piece of fielding I ever saw at cover point was by Clive Lloyd in an International Cavaliers match. The ball was hit wide of his right hand, I was fielding extra cover and could see that there was no way I was going to get to it. Suddenly Clive Lloyd appeared like a big cat, with an outstretched telescopic arm that stopped the ball, falling over as he did so, and all in one movement he rolled, threw the ball in and ran out the striker, who was trying to get back, by two yards. I would like to see more emphasis on teaching young cricketers to field properly. Fielding in itself can provide a very exciting aspect of the game.

The greatest fielder I ever knew caught everything and had to be sent home half way through the series.

The best catcher close to the wicket on the leg side was Tony Lock of Surrey and England. Alan Davidson of Australia was another great fielder, who became known as the Claw. The two best slip fielders were Bobby Simpson of Australia and Phil Sharpe of Yorkshire and England. It was once said about Bobby that during a conversation with Wally Grout the Australian keeper, the bowler bowled, the batsman got an edge, Bobby leaned to his right, caught the ball, threw it back and carried on the conversation without missing a word. Philip Sharpe used to catch the ball behind him by letting it pass first. He said it gave him more time. Colin Cowdrey was a good slip, he would put the ball in his pocket and nobody would know where it was.

To be a good slip fielder you must concentrate on every single ball and have what is known as soft hands. That doesn't mean that the outside of the skin is soft. It means that you let the ball come to you before trying to catch it. Too many slip fielders in club cricket and even in county cricket tend to snatch at the ball.

With the advent of inswing bowling the first and most brilliant of short legs was Ernie Wise.

Brian Close and Philip Sharpe were vying for a fielding prize of £100 or something similar, for the most catches in the season. Only two or three catches separated them and with a couple of

GOT OFF LIGHT THIS MORNING, CLOSEY?

matches to go we were playing against Gloucester at Bristol. Philip Sharpe was in his normal position at first slip and Closey was fielding just in front of square. Raymond Illingworth was bowling and suddenly he bowled his seamer. He used to use this regularly on non-turning wickets and would swing it away from the batsman, pitching it about leg

WHAT?

stump. If he pitched it right the batsman would try to lap the ball and more often than not he would get a wicket. This day Martin Young was the batsman for Gloucester and he went down on one knee and played the sweep shot and hit the ball beautifully, bang in the middle of the bat. It hit Closey on the forehead straight between the eyes. The ball bounced from his head over the top of a startled Martin Young, over the top of Jimmy Binks our wicket keeper, to Philip Sharpe at first slip, who gratefully caught it. I will never forget the look on Closey's face. He gave Philip the biggest bollocking of his life, for even attempting to claim it as a catch from off his head. Closey played bloody hell for ten minutes before eventually asking the scorers if he could claim the catch. In the finish he was quite ready to settle and call it half a piece.

Running Between The Wickets

Run outs occur quite often and always will — mix-ups in the heat of the moment we all know about. Batsmen are taught there are three distinct calls, 'no', 'yes' and 'wait'. Of course nobody can rely on this. There is many a time when batsmen just look at each other and they know it's a run, especially if they have been batting together for a long time. They know each other's habits. Len Hutton once said to the press, after he had run out Denis Compton in a Test match, 'When you run with Denis, you don't shout, you pray'.

Talking about run outs reminds me of the occasion when an average county player wanting one run to complete his century replied with a sharp 'no' when called for one by his partner, a Test player regarded as a good judge of the quick single. At the end of the over the England man walked up the wicket and said, 'I reckon I'm the best judge of a run in this county so when I say run you run.' 'That's as may be, came the reply, 'but when I'm 99 not out I reckon I'm the best judge of a run in the whole bloody world'.

In India, if you are running between the wickets you have got to have a runner like Brendan Foster just in case the curry is too hot.

Calling between the wickets is very important and George Emmett who was the captain of Gloucester-shire and opening bat, found himself batting with Bomber Wells who was number eleven. Bomber was not the greatest batsman in the world. Like

Mick Cowan of Yorkshire, he thought the only reason he took a bat in was to save you running 22 yards. After Bomber had pushed one into the covers and set off for a run, he stopped, and walked back. George Emmett had set off wanting to get the bowling, got half way down, finished up turning round and diving back into his crease and got covered in dirt and muck. He brushed himself down and walked up the wicket to Bomber and said, 'Bomber, when we are batting together for God's sake call'. So Bomber said, 'Heads'.

At Gloucester on one occasion George Emmett said to Sam Cook and Tom Goddard, 'If there are any more run outs between you two, the one that's at fault is going to have a week off without pay. You are both capable of getting a few runs to help the side. Instead you keep getting run out.' It so happened in one match that both Sam Cook and Tom Goddard were injured and Gloucestershire, wanting a few runs, sent them both out with runners. The biggest cock up of all time took place and all four finished up at one end. They ran off the field, up the pavilion steps, waving their bats at the crowd – one of the many funny sights ever seen on a cricket field.

Sometimes batsmen are injured and they have to have a runner, I remember one match in Lancashire where one of the batsmen had to run for the other whilst he limped all day. Eventually the injured man got to 99 and, I heard, that when he pushed the ball for a single he beat his runner to the other end by three yards!

My Captains

Possibly the best county captain I played under would be Norman Yardley. His knowledge of the game and reading of the wicket had to be seen to be believed. There were times when rain affected the wicket and he would say, 'Ah! it's too wet for the moment for the roller. I think we are alright batting on that for another two to three hours. When it starts to dry I think the problems will start so let's make sure that the other side are batting at that time.' We had to get on with it. For a leader of men I think that Ronnie Burnett, an old former Yorkshire Captain, must rank as the best. He took over the side that in 1958 was ravished and torn apart with silly internal squabbles. He got some youngsters with a few old pros, moulded them together, and in 1959 that same side, with a great team spirit of one for all and all for one, won the County Championship. For me it was a great performance. For boldness Brian Close took the biscuit. He would stand ridiculously close to the wicket and never ask anyone to do anything that he was afraid to do.

The best Test captain I have played under was a professional, Len Hutton. His knowledge of the game was absolutely fantastic. The manipulation of his bowlers was tremendous. To be fair he had people like Tyson, Statham, Loader, Trueman, Lock, Laker, Wardle, Appleyard at his command. Not all at once! Can you imagine that line up of bowlers? Bowlers who would bowl any side out on any wicket with a captain who knew how to use them, especially me. He used to bowl me in very short spells and if I had bowled 25 overs at the end of the day, I felt almost as fresh as I did in the morning, better sometimes. The best amateur captain I played under was without doubt Peter May, a man with boyish looks underneath which was a killer instinct.

An off the field captain has a greater responsibility than the on-field captain – he has got to prove to the rest of the team that he can get as drunk as they can.

Famous Captains No I

N. F. Grass-Zeppelin seen here going down on a notorious "sticky dog"

Umpires

The umpire has one of the worst jobs in cricket. It's a job I wouldn't want and yet it is a fact that most of our umpires are former players – men who played the game for many years and who know the laws inside out. For them it is more than a job, it's a way of life. I have no hesitation in saying that the best umpires in the world are to be found in English cricket. Part of the reason for this lies in the fact that we play much more cricket. There simply isn't enough cricket played abroad to provide umpires with the experience needed to make a top class Test umpire. Mark you, there will never be a perfect umpire. How can you please the bowler and the batsmen on the same decision? That's the important word – decision, because that's what the umpire does all the time – make decisions. One thing I like about cricket is that you rarely see players arguing with umpires over decisions. There will always be the odd player who shows dissent even so.

Some batsmen have a bad attitude when they are given out by an umpire, whether it's caught behind or lbw. Some don't like getting out. Some bowlers don't like being hit for four – it's all part of the game. But I can tell all batsmen and bowlers it's no use arguing with the umpire. If you don't believe me, try standing in the position of an umpire in any match. From his viewpoint he gets the best sighting of any delivery. The batsman will probably have moved a little bit after the ball has hit his leg, not knowing that he has done so in the heat of the moment. Even a bowler, when he has delivered, might feel that he has pitched on, but as he has thrown himself away from the wicket in his follow through he has completely lost the line of where the ball pitched. The umpire's view is the best, that is why he is put there. I know I got blamed many times for words with umpires, but I can honestly say I never turned round and bollocked one in my life. He has a hard job to do.

English batsmen tend to walk if they get a nick and are caught behind because they believe in trying to help the umpire a little bit. I think they should. A lot of old players you talk to who played before the war say that it is wrong. They say that umpires are there to do a job and if they do it badly, then they shouldn't be in the position. I would like to see how good some of them would be making decisions on doubtful matters every day.

If a batsman hits the ball to the keeper and knows it and doesn't walk, to me he is cheating. He wouldn't stay at the wicket if he hit the ball to mid-on so why should he if he knows he has hit it behind. The batsmen abroad, especially Australians and West Indians, don't believe in walking at all. That could have something to do with the very bad standard of their umpiring. The umpire's job is

YOU'RE THE WRONG END, SUNBEAM!

hard enough, so, when captaining a side, I would always give credit to those umpires who had the courage of their conviction. I marked down the 'iffers' who can't quite make their minds up. I don't rate any umpire top class if the finger goes straight up following a shout, unless it is really obvious. I do rate the umpire, especially in an lbw decision, who takes his time to think about it for a moment to replay a mental picture before he gives a decision.

I remember Freddie getting a batsman caught behind, and after the umpire had given him out a woman in the crowd shouted, 'Kill the umpire, kill the umpire'. We only found out after the game that it was the umpire's wife.

When I was a young man playing cricket for Yorkshire and England there was, in the game, one of the loveliest characters cricket has ever known, a man by the name of Alec Skelding, who became an umpire. The lads called him Doc Skelding because he used to carry his old cricket boots in a

OH! UMPIRES ?

bowls bag and wear them when he stood as umpire, with his own white coat and his white hat. We really loved the old boy. One day in 1948 Alec was umpiring a match at Northampton between Northamptonshire and Australia. Australia won the toss and batted. The first over was bowled by Nobby Clark who then played for Northampton, fast left-arm over the wicket. Australia opened with Syd Barnes and Bill Brown, Syd Barnes being a bit of a volatile character – a very good player, especially off his legs through the mid-wicket and the mid-on area. Anyway, umpire Skelding gave his guard one leg, and after looking round the field said, 'play'. Nobby Clark proceeded to bowl the first over and at about the fourth ball he swung one in a bit late and Syd Barnes, playing it through mid-wicket, missed it.

dog is', said Alec, 'I've got rid of him for yapping, like I'm getting rid of thee, now bugger off.'

I remember once when Freddie was bowling and the batsman got a snick on the ball, the first slip caught it and the umpire said, 'Not out'. The next ball Freddie bowled, the wicket keeper caught it and the umpire said, 'Not out'. The next ball Freddie shouted 'how's that', for an lbw, and the umpire said, 'Not out'. The next ball Fred took the middle stump 25 yards back and he shouted at the umpire 'that must have been bloody close'.

There was a fine old character – Bill Reeves. He was once umpiring at Lord's and R. W. V. Robins the Middlesex captain was bowling his leg spinners and was not having a very good day. As you probably know the emblem of the Middlesex sweater is three scimitars. At the end of the over, having turned down a couple of shouts, Bill turned to R. W. V. Robins and said, 'Would you like your sweater Sir?' Robins said, 'No, you can stick it right up your backside'. Bill replied, 'What, swords an' all?' Some of the best umpires in my time at home must surely have been Frank Chester, Frank Lee, Syd Buller and Charlie Elliot.

I used to be a very good cricketer until my eyes went, and then I became an umpire.

There is no shortage of personalities today either. One who immediately comes to mind is a character by the name of Dickie Bird. Dickie, who played for Yorkshire and Leicester, is a bundle of nervous energy as anyone who has seen him signal a boundary will know. We also have one of the great talkers in the game, one Master William Alley, the Australian. But for me no one will ever quite replace old Doc Skelding.

I remember once when bowling against George Dawkes of Derbyshire I tried to bowl a yorker and I hit him on the top of the instep. It was a very painful blow with a newish ball. I appealed for lbw to Alec Skelding shouting, 'How is he?' and Alec said quickly, 'I bet he bloody hurts and he's out as well'.

The best umpire I have ever played with abroad, believe me, was a Chinaman, by the name of Lee Kow who came from Trinidad. We thought he was so good that during the Tour of 1959 to 1960, our

The ball hit him on the pads and they do say that Alec Skelding appealed as well. Syd Barnes had no chance, old Alec put his finger up and said, in his own way, 'Thou's out'. Syd Barnes said, 'I'm what? You must be joking'. 'You're out', said Alec. As Syd passed him on his way back to the pavilion he whispered, 'Where's your white stick Alec and where's your guide dog?' 'I'll tell you where the

manager R. W. V. Robins asked if he could be brought to Jamaica to umpire the Test match there.

We do have one or two Australian umpires standing in English cricket. On one occasion during an Australia v Yorkshire match at Bradford, one of these umpires gave Greg Chappell out on what can only be described as a doubtful caught behind. At lunch time when the umpires returned to the pavilion, Greg had a word with his fellow countryman and said, 'I was nowhere near that one', and the umpire replied, 'I know, but there are 15,000 Yorkshiremen out there and only three Australians'.

In the league some of the umpires are absolutely dreadful. They do get certificates and they talk about it as though it gives them the Lord's right. Putting something on paper and then doing it in reality is a completely different thing. Some of the decisions I have seen when I have watched or played league cricket have been beyond the ridiculous. You always get the umpire in the league who is going to let you know that he is the gaffer and when you get one of these you've had it. I have seen league cricket officials get a bloke who was sitting in the stand to umpire when they have been short. He's straight on with the jacket and within ten minutes he's taken over the whole match. He knows nothing about the game and decisions are flying left, right and centre. Sometimes this can be a very big disadvantage, especially for youngsters. Particularly

those who are trying to get into the team. Bad umpiring can break their confidence. How about the league bowler who shouted, 'How is he, dad?' and the umpire replied, 'That is definitely out, son'. It would be a good thing to pay league umpires substantial amounts for giving up their Saturdays, particularly if we could get old county players or even minor county players to go into league cricket. It would do good at the grass roots of the game, where, let's face it, our youngsters and stars of tomorrow have to come from.

Off the field of play the umpire is usually a very friendly sort of character. In fact, you do find some umpires staying in the same hotel as the players. The game is forgotten, they talk about cricket generally, nearly all of the time. When you get cricketers together they do tend to talk about cricket, I think it's marvellous. Umpires and players can swap yarns and different ideas and talk about what is good for the game from their different points of view. As far as the players are concerned the umpires are a very important part of the game and the relationship is a good one. In fact I have heard players talk to umpires about the way they were out that day – what they did, what they would have to do not to do it again. Usually the umpire will tell them. It's like bowling, the umpire will sometimes tell you when you are getting a little bit close to the front line. Things like this, little tips,

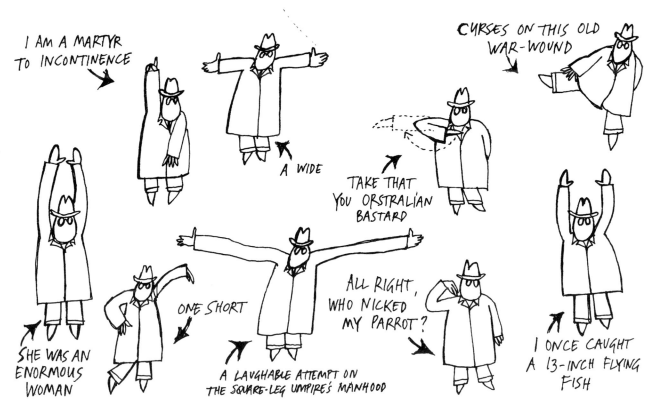

I AM A MARTYR TO INCONTINENCE

A WIDE

CURSES ON THIS OLD WAR-WOUND

TAKE THAT YOU ORSTRALIAN BASTARD

SHE WAS AN ENORMOUS WOMAN

ONE SHORT

ALL RIGHT, WHO NICKED MY PARROT?

A LAUGHABLE ATTEMPT ON THE SQUARE-LEG UMPIRE'S MANHOOD

I ONCE CAUGHT A 13-INCH FLYING FISH

WHICH WAY IS MECCA?

RED CARPET MARK I

held a grudge. When one of their star players came in to bat he said to the bowler, 'Look at this cocky little so and so, he thinks he's a great player.' The old bowler thought to himself, 'He doesn't seem to like this fellow, if I hit him somewhere on the pads I'm going to keep shouting.' Sure enough the second ball he bowled he hit the batsman on the pad, shouted loud and the umpire gave him out. You can't blame the bowler, but you must the umpire.

It is said that in Australia when Queensland were trying to get into the Sheffield Shield Competition they had a batsman who could get them there if he was able to stay at the wicket. Two old umpires were fully aware of this and as the fellow was batting he was caught behind. The yell that went up could be heard all over Queensland, but the umpire gave him not out. He was eventually hit on the pad in front of the wickets, plumb lbw and that was given not out. He was even caught at gully off a full blooded slash and the umpire shouted, 'no ball', almost after the catch. After he had made a hundred he went down the track, missed the ball, and the old wicket keeper took the bails off and removed all three stumps. He turned to the umpire and said, 'We'll just have a couple of quid that the bastard's out this time.'

Cec Pepper, an Australian who has been umpiring in England for many years now, was standing at Scarborough during a festival match when I was bowling down the bank. I appealed for an lbw and he turned me down. The very next ball I appealed again, perhaps a bit louder and again he turned me down. The third time I shouted so loudly that it left him no alternative but to shout back at me, 'Not out'. I, in return, said, 'Why not?' and he said, 'Because there are three stumps at that end not a row of bloody palings.'

Festival cricket is normally played at places like Scarborough and Morecambe. I come from Morecambe. It's not my real name, my real name is Blackpool, but Scarborough is the actual home for festival cricket. Everybody plays and everybody likes each other and everyone is very friendly towards each other.

Even so I don't think there is such a thing as a friendly game of cricket. In competitive sport there cannot be any friendliness on the field. Afterwards yes, but I think the game on the field must be played hard. If Derek Underwood is bowling and the ball is taking spin it doesn't matter who is in. Whether it's the Queen of England, Prince Philip, Prince Charles, Ted Dexter or any royalty, he is going to try to get them out; and that is the spirit of cricket – not gin as some cricketers would have you think.

which I think are all for the good of the game.

You get to the point where you know your umpires, you know who will give 'out' and who will give 'not out'. Some bowlers get very crafty and work on these facts. I did hear of an umpire who played for a certain county and got the sack and

The Twelfth Man

One of the worst things that can happen to a cricketer is to be told he is the twelfth man. A player bordering on selection has to suffer this agony at the beginning of every match. Having received the disappointing news that he is twelfth man he knows that it's his lot to be general team valet for the next three days. (This is only two days in a Test match because you are allowed to join your county side on Saturday for a Championship match if you are not selected.) If a player wants lunch in the dressing-room because he hasn't the time to get changed to go to the dining room before the next session, the twelfth man has got to get his meal. He also has to get all the autograph books and the bats signed, he takes drinks onto the field, phones in bets, rings girl friends and fields if anyone comes off. Some twelfth men in fact have been known to field right throughout the match – in some instances for both sides. It's difficult for a captain if a twelfth man is fielding regularly because he gets used to him on the field and if the man happens to be a bowler, might well want to put him on. This did happen in a county match at Derbyshire when their captain back in the 1940s, E. J. Gothard, tried to bowl Eric Marsh. The players let him set the field before they told him. I suppose one can say that the twelfth man is the professional lackey, not a very nice job, but some players I have met have been quite happy to be that just to be part of the side. It is the most disheartening thing I know to be told in a Test match or even a county match, that you are the one to be left out.

When Fred got married he hurt his arm and his leg, so they sent the twelfth man on honeymoon to do his duty.

Wickets

I noticed how, compared with my early days in 1949, by the 1960s when I retired, the pitches had started to get slower and slower. I think this could have been something ordered by committees to groundsmen on the basis that they hadn't quick bowlers in their side, or due to over loaming. Little seamers, or in the words of the lads, phantoms, started to appear in the game. This is where I think the English standard started its downward trend.

All the bowlers did was to run up off six, seven or eight yards, bowl straight on a length and move the ball a little bit either way. They set defensive fields and sweated the batsmen out. I'm sure I saw the decline of the game start then. I think it was because of the phantom seamer that slow wickets became accepted and created the beginning of the end for the leg spin bowlers. I also think that it brought into the game bat and pad defensive techniques which can clearly be seen when you watch players now. They always play with the bat and pad extremely close together. This is where I would go back to the lbw rule because the batsman is unable to get onto the back foot with confidence knowing that, if the ball has pitched six inches outside the off-stump, he will not be in a position to play an attacking shot for fear of being out lbw.

Slow wickets have also been the beginning of the end for the slow bowlers who flighted the ball or gave it air. Suddenly we started seeing slow bowlers bowling with a very flat trajectory. This in turn also helped to stamp out one of the best sights in cricket, that of the batsman using his feet to get to the pitch of a slow bowler and turn it into a half volley. Spinners now bowl so quick with this flat trajectory that the Victor Trumper type of approach – another aspect of the game which was always exciting to the spectators – has vanished. I think there is far too much fertiliser used on wickets in preparation. I have to be careful what I'm saying here, because I've never actually prepared a wicket. But I know I can take you to grounds where, if you lie down at ground level on your tummy and look to the square, you can see how it sits up like a plateau. Sometimes it's as high as two feet above the level of the rest of the ground. I often wonder if at the present moment in England we are actually playing on natural soil or whether they are marl and fertiliser beds.

Weather and Cover

The covering of wickets I find totally inadequate at times. Just covers placed over the pitch, and in most cases the square itself is left to the elements. Many times the wicket is fit to play but the surrounds are not. Old wickets, where ends have been doctored badly by the groundsmen, apart from looking very unsightly cause most of the problems. Many is the time that rain stands on top of the square because the square has been rolled too hard. The water can't get through because the groundsmen haven't forked the area. It is certainly something that wants looking at in the near future.

On a lot of grounds in England I find the ground equipment inadequate. It doesn't deal with the elements well enough. Many is the time I have thought that with better equipment games could have got under way much quicker and often even been finished. 'If this had been a club match we would have been playing now', is a statement I have heard often. But when players are playing for their living, their bread and butter, the conditions have to be right otherwise it is not fair. Mind you, I sympathise with the spectators because they want to see play. Sometimes even with the sun shining the players are playing cards in the dressing-room. We can get to the bloody moon now, but we still can't seem to cover a wicket properly. Many is the time I have felt sorry for the public, who pay their money with no guarantee of play, and if there is none they don't get their money back. Actually there have been occasions recently when people, quite rightly, have asked for their money back, because no play has taken place. It is something that the game will have to look closely at. Another bad thing that occurs is that when play starts late, sometimes because of bad weather, a full session is not always played. Having started at one o'clock players take their lunch within the hour. I think if play does start that late a full two hours should be played to give the crowd something for their money. This would certainly help to sooth any bad feeling and care should be taken to encourage more interest. If grounds were properly covered spectators would turn up in doubtful weather knowing that play would take place if it wasn't raining. The conditions abroad are completely different. They have summer in their summers. They are not reliant on the weather as much as we are in England. If it rains abroad the first thing the ground staff do is to pull a great big square tarpaulin sheet right over the whole square, so that the elements do not affect the ground. It is fortunate that the rain also goes through the ground much quicker in dryer conditions than in England. Once it has stopped raining the tarpaulin sheets are rolled back and you can guarantee that within a quarter of an hour the game is on again.

Players in the north of England say that it's a pity that the fixtures can't be drawn up for them to be able to play in the south of England for at least the first three and the last three weeks of the season. A lot feel that playing in the north of England is a handicap because of the weather. Yorkshire have won a few Championships in spite of it. I know many bowlers who when batting first on a good wicket hope it will throw it down with rain overnight, especially on uncovered wickets, so that they have an advantage over the other side. I have always thought this to be a weak attitude to adopt, because if you are going to be a top class player you must be able to bowl people out on good cricket. It's why we are not only a nation of shop-wickets. Good wickets are the greatest training ground for any bowler. It makes them think. It makes them try things that they wouldn't dream of trying if everything was going their way. The unpredictable weather in England doesn't help our keepers. but medium-paced seamers as well.

I COULD HAVE SWORN THEY SAID 'DOCTOR THE WICKET-KEEPER'

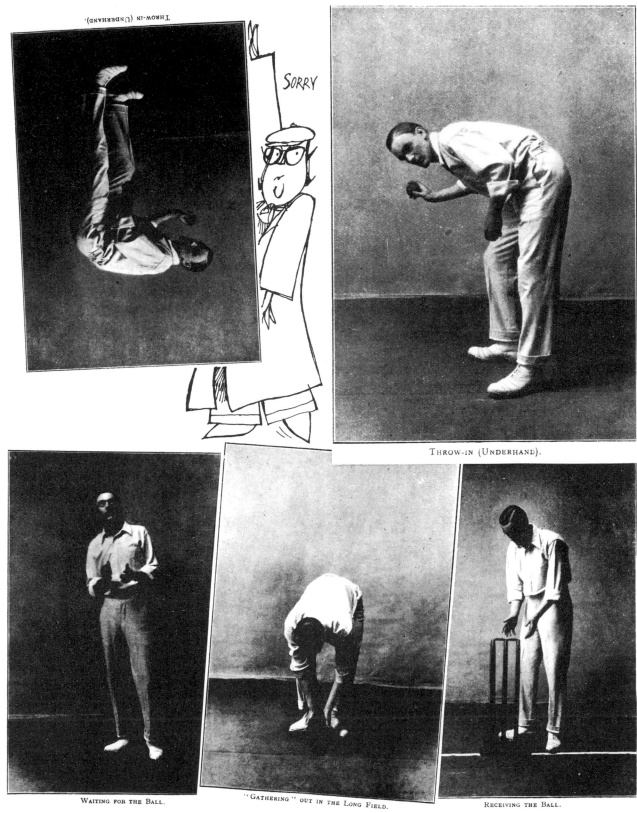

THROW-IN (UNDERHAND).

SORRY

THROW-IN (UNDERHAND).

WAITING FOR THE BALL.

"GATHERING" OUT IN THE LONG FIELD.

RECEIVING THE BALL.

At the Grass Roots

THOUGHTS ON THE LEAST PUBLICISED ACTIVITIES IN THE GAME OF CRICKET

Coaching

Bad coaching has always been a failing of English cricket. The reason, primarily, is that cricket is once again trying to get things on the cheap. I have always believed that in England we have the best coaches money can buy, but if we are going to ask them to do a proper job, they have got to be paid a proper wage. I'm not talking about £3000 per year. These are people who have played for 20 years or more and have given their life to the game and know what it's all about. They have all the knowledge and technique available to pass on to youngsters. We should never find ourselves in the position of having only one world class batsman in our national side – Boycott. We should set up a proper coaching system throughout England — and I don't mean with school teachers and amateurs who have played the game a little bit. We want professionals, ex-players who are paid a wage in the region of £7-8000, with a car and expenses to travel around the counties looking for and training talent.

Some coaches ask me to look at players because they think they may be able to bowl a bit. The first thing I see is a run up which is obviously not right. The man is unbalanced, there is no rhythm, he comes charging up at the same speed all the way. In fact you see some of them slowing up when they get to the wicket, when they should be accelerating or at least maintaining their pace. Some I find bowling completely square on when the ball can go only one way, and that is in. There are occasions when I am asked to have a look at a young man because it is thought he might bat a bit, and as soon as he takes up his stance, I can see there is something wrong because he is batting chest on. There have been very few batsmen with a two-eyed stance that were successful. Basically, we should drill into our players and top class coaches that this game is sideways on, whether you are batting, bowling or fielding.

I am appalled when I meet many old players who have left the game and taken all their knowledge, their know-how and technique with them, never to return to the game again.

It is no use the press or the authorities saying that we are struggling to find talent. Cricket is the national game of England and talent has been available for over three centuries.

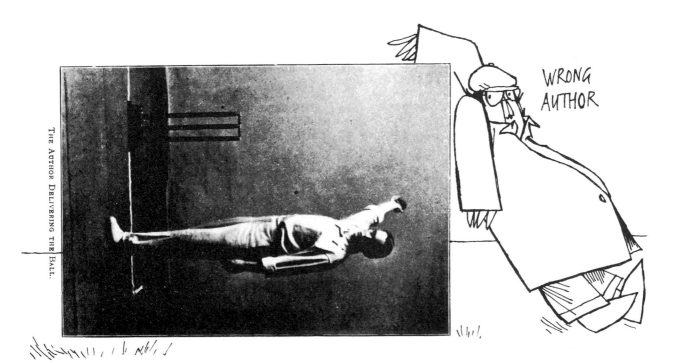

THE AUTHOR DELIVERING THE BALL.

WRONG AUTHOR

There is never enough money to promote youth sport in Britain. We don't even have an amateur football team with any standing in the world. Any club can come over and beat us purely and simply because there is not enough money put into the training of the game. Cricket and football suffer from a lack of direct income to put into youth development. Dennis Howell can turn round and say that we put £300,000 back into football and £7 back into cricket, and he's a friend of mine — at least he was, but that's not enough. The socialist government should be more like their brothers the Russians and have fortunes ploughed back into our game. You cannot make a success with a cup of tea on a village green, a cup of tea and a crumpet. If you're lucky with the crumpet you can, but not with the tea. Society today requires healthy success. The need to encourage school cricket and youth cricket is tremendous. But well-meaning people are hampered by insufficient funds.

Net practice is used in the main by players wanting to warm up, to get a sight of the ball, to get their timing right and to iron out any bad faults that they may have accumulated during early play, or during a lay off. Nets should be used by batsmen as serious practice and not as an opportunity to go in and throw the bat at every ball. Strong coaches would make them play correctly. They would be forced to play shots that they are not playing as well as they think they ought to, to get the feel of them. Bowlers should be asked to bowl to the batsmen's weaknesses, enabling the maximum amount of practice. Nets are important to youngsters. They enable the coach to spend a lot of time teaching them the basic points of the game, because without them there is nothing to build on. There is no use sending your youngster to the nets automatically expecting him to come back like Don Bradman and then blaming the coach because he doesn't. If the talent is there, it can be brought out and improved, but if it is not there, forget it, no one can put talent in.

Talking about nets, when I went to the nets in Yorkshire in 1948, it was described then as an exceptional year for Yorkshire cricket. As many as 614 boys were invited to attend, and at the beginning of the summer the Yorkshire coaches chose three players who they thought might make county cricketers. They were Brian Close, Frank Lowson and myself. There was a fourth, but they were not quite sure that he would make the grade. He was Ray Illingworth. In those days it was Ray's batting that they were looking at, not his off-spin bowling, because Raymond went to the nets as a batsman

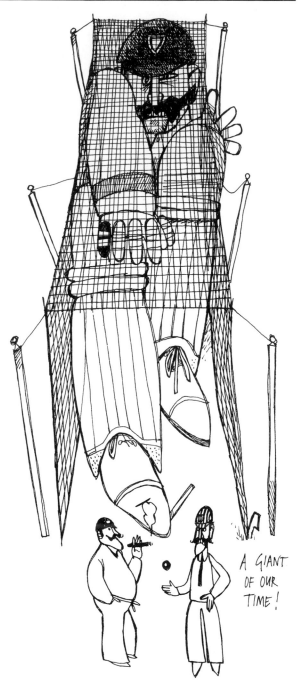

A GIANT OF OUR TIME!

and medium-paced new ball bowler. I remember Ray getting four wickets in a Test match against New Zealand at Leeds, bowling seamers. In fact he was dropped for the next match. There have been times when Yorkshire have had 500 boys at the nets. Afterwards we would sit and talk and the coaches would say, 'Well, we've got 500 here but we don't think that we have seen one that will get above minor county level.' It is said that 1 in 1000 becomes a county cricketer, something like 1 in 5000 makes it to international level.

School Cricket

I have developed a big interest in school cricket and I find when I go to state schools that I am appalled by the lack of facilities for our sportsmen of the future. Not many schools have cricket grounds, rugby grounds, athletic pitches or the like, which cannot be good. I do take great pride in visiting our public schools where they usually have wonderful facilities. I think cricket has been particularly good to me and I enjoy putting something back by playing against these boys. It gets me out in the fresh air for a day, and I must admit that even when bowling against a 16 or 17-year-old, I still get a great thrill if the ball pitches somewhere around middle stump and hits the top of the off — or even if I beat the bat. One of the reasons why I give so much time to schools cricket is, like many old players, I want to be able to sit down in the future, when I am too old to play, and be able to watch cricket and enjoy it. After all it has been my life. I think it's only right that I try to teach kids how to hold the bat, how to bowl, how to get their feet in the right position, how to set a proper attacking field. But above all I would like to make sure that I teach youngsters to learn to enjoy the game by playing it well.

Club Cricket

Club cricket is something I know little about, not having played it for many years. But let's face it, it's club cricket that provides the grounding for our future county and Test players. Without club cricket there wouldn't be league cricket, without league cricket there wouldn't be county cricket, and certainly not international cricket. Although it does a great job, there are one or two things that I would criticise, perhaps the most important of all is the standard of club wickets. They ought to be much better for youngsters to play on. If a boy gets hit in the mouth with a hard ball, his confidence can be shattered. I would like to see the NCC through the NCA, the National Cricket Association, organise the clubs better in ground preparation.* To my mind, it would certainly improve the overall standard of club cricket in England if the wickets were better. It's one of the things I've noticed abroad, the wickets the club players play on are far better than those that ours are generally subjected to. The weather has a lot to do with this and I would imagine also finance, but you can't build a brick wall well without a plumbline.

The NCC sounds like a ventriloquist who is a member of the MCC.

League Cricket

League cricket is of course very different from club cricket. League cricket is much more competitive, they play to win a league, play to win various trophies and cups and perhaps the most important of all – they play to win. League cricket is very strong in the north of England, where the very big leagues are. It is not unusual for international professionals to be employed and this means that the league players do have the opportunity to play against world class players, every weekend. Watching and playing against good players I always reckon is the best way to success. I've always said, that to improve yourself in any game, you must play against the best players available. Try to get into a good league side and use that as a springboard to get into minor county or county second team cricket. This will eventually, if you are good enough, take you into county cricket. County cricket in Yorkshire is the ultimate. A lot of players compete for the honour, just to be able to say that they played for their county. If they play in only one

or two matches they believe that they have achieved a goal. If they walk out in a county side, it puts them in good standing in league cricket and builds a bit of reputation for them. I must admit though that sometimes in league cricket, county reputations stand for nothing and league cricketers let county cricketers know about it. I would say, without doubt, that every Yorkshire father whose son shows the promise of playing cricket, looks forward to the day when he will possibly play for his county and wear a Yorkshire cap. It is still the done thing for Yorkshiremen to have their pregnant wives driven up the M1 or M6 to make sure that the child is born in Yorkshire, in the hopes that if it's a boy at least he will qualify to play for the county. As everyone knows, we are the only county who still stick to the rule, that a player must be born within the county boundaries to be allowed to play for the county. Be born twenty yards outside and, unfortunately, you have missed out and could be Lancashire's gain.

Benefit Matches

Until a few years ago, before the Sunday League was formed, it was always an accepted thing that cricketers taking their hard-earned benefits after ten years' service, would arrange a series of Sunday matches. These would be played in different parts of their counties when sides like my own, Yorkshire, were visiting. The opposition did all they could to help swell the funds of a man's benefit. It meant so much to him, to his wife, to his children and to his whole future. In fact the benefit can help a man retain his standard of living once finishing with cricket. It is very hard to come out of the game at somewhere near 38 or 40 and suddenly try to find a job that suits, especially in the economic climate we now find ourselves in. The John Player Sunday League stopped these benefit matches from taking place and there are only three or four Sundays when this can now be done.

I always think that it was through benefits that the game became so closely linked with the world of show business. A lot of big names like Harry Secombe, Eric Morecambe, Willie Rushton, Leslie Crowther, and film stars such as Trevor Howard and John Mills, have turned out in benefit matches. I have seen Syd James, Tony Hancock, David Tomlinson, Ian Carmichael and hosts of others playing cricket on Sundays. I am asked why show business people like to play and watch the game so much. I think it is because show business people work at night in clubs and on the stage, so during the day when they have rested there is nothing nicer than slipping along to a cricket match, sitting in the sunshine, possibly having a drink, relaxing and watching the game. Many stars put on benefit nights in clubs up and down the country for different players. Dave Allen and Leslie Crowther in particular, do this kind of thing. It's great to see how much the players are appreciated by these people. Trevor Howard has a passionate love for the game of cricket. He is a Member of the MCC and if he is making a film, it's said, that it is written into his contract that the week of the Test match at Lord's is the week that he has off! It was with benefits that the International Cavaliers did such a great job. They got players from all over the world to play in Sunday matches for very nice fees to benefit the beneficiary. But because it became so popular and attracted the crowds, as I have mentioned, it was pinched by the hierarchy. Many players' benefits have been more than doubled by having the International Cavaliers, and I know they were grateful.

Charity Cricket

One of the advantages that cricket has against rugby or football, or the majority of other sports, is the tremendous amount of work it is able to do for charity. I am the President of the Lord's Taverners and our cricket is played every Sunday throughout the summer all over the country, and we make a tremendous amount of money for our charities. The advantage is that we can play a team of firemen or whoever, and two people, usually stars, may well be batting. The rest of the. team are off the pitch, signing autographs, having their photographs taken and chatting to the crowd. Now in football all the stars are on at once and the public get an hour-and-a-half of not very good entertainment. Most of the stars can't play. It is obvious a lot of them don't want to play and a lot of them are not fit enough to. To play charity cricket you don't have to be fit – look at Fred, either one. You are on show for about four to five hours. Many celebrities support the Lord's Taverners. There are too many here to mention, but thank you all the same.

In addition to celebrities from stage, screen and radio there are also a lot of old retired players playing for Lord's Taverners in Sunday matches. I don't think there is any other sport in Britain that does as much for charity as cricket does. There are other personalities who are very good at after dinner speaking. They attend dinners and functions for charities.

C. Freud having his minced morsels attended to.

They do it quite willingly with no jousting to persuade them to arrive. I give books and cricket bats which I get autographed throughout the season and send personal items to charity every year. Yet I still get letters from people asking why I haven't had time to bother about their particular organisation. I must say that the charities I tend to become more involved with nowadays work for children or youngsters, particularly those under-privileged.

I remember Leslie Crowther speaking in Yorkshire on one occasion when Harold Wilson and Brian Clough were on the same speakers' bill. Leslie Crowther, overawed by this, on standing to introduce himself, said, 'Mr Chairman, Gentlemen, you just cannot appreciate the honour that you have bestowed on me this evening. You have given me, a mere mortal, the opportunity of speaking before the Lord God Almighty and his only begotten Son.'

The Lord's Taverners give a tremendous amount of money to youth cricket and youth in general. They have recently started to provide coaches for under-privileged children. All is given quite freely and with a lot of love. In 1978 we are expecting to make in the region of £120,000 of which, I think, £32 goes straight back into cricket and the rest is on the bar bill.

I don't know why it is, but there is a great association between cricketers and people in show business, like Eric, Harry Secombe, Willie, John Alderton, Tom Baker and all the many others who play in charity matches. I used to play with that great guy Harry Secombe at a ground in Surrey. A lot of England boys used to play there and Harry would get stars of the stage, screen and radio to appear with them. I was playing on Harry's side one year with a terrific crowd in the ground when Pete Murray, another great mate of mine, came in to bat. Harry said to me, let him have one off the proper run up but outside the off-stump. For God's sake don't try to hit him. I said, 'Don't worry, Harry, I'll do it for you.' So I marked the run up and Pete said, 'Eh! What's going off?' and Harry said, 'He's going to let you have it.' 'But he's a mate of mine', said Pete. 'He's still going to let you have it', Harry said, so he sent the slips farther back. Well we had a fellow by the name of Eric Sykes, keeping wicket. What a lovely man and good comedian he is, but he is a little deaf, and of course Harry, having given instructions, forgot that Eric was a bit deaf and as I came racing into the wicket and let one go outside the off-stump I suddenly noticed that Eric hadn't moved! The ball really flashed through and Pete Murray had hardly moved his foot let alone his bat, and with Harry Secombe roaring with laughter and saying to Pete, 'Come on Pete Murray, you are on 45's not 33's', the ball reached Eric Sykes and he was only about six yards back! I remember the whole scene so well. Eric tried to take the ball and shouted as the ball, his gloves and he were all up in the air at the same time, and as he came down he broke his finger. Poor old Eric. But worse was to follow. He was playing a guitar part in a film and they do tell me, I don't know how true it is, that the film had to be put back nearly two-and-a-half weeks while Eric's finger mended.

One of my personal friends, not a cricketer as such, because he is a professional footballer, is Malcolm Macdonald. I have known Malcolm for many years now and he loves the game of cricket. He is very bow-legged and I once saw him playing in a charity cricket match. He looked just like the bite from a white doughnut. As a matter of fact he didn't play very much that day because we hung him on the dressing-room door for luck. Of course good cricket players, like Malcolm's legs, are few and far between!

The President of an organisation like the Lord's Taverners, or any other organisation working for charity, has to speak at dinners and lunches. Now this, I must be perfectly honest, I find difficult to do.

I do it because it is a challenge. I always give the impression that I can make a speech up as I go along. I can't – I have prepared and rehearsed it for days. It is one of the hardest things that I have to do. In fact I sweat when I get prepared. There are people, of course, who actually enjoy speaking – Freddie in particular, he is a very good talker, he never stops. The Canon Jackson from Blackburn, he is also a marvellous speaker. With me being a professional the audience expects a little bit more, so I have to work that little bit harder. Although the Canon is a professional, when he stands up, he tells you about cricket and gives you a sermon at the same time, which is absolutely fantastic. Prince Philip is a good speaker. Prince Charles is a good speaker. Princess Anne is a good speaker, and it's like I said to the Queen the other day, I can't stand name droppers. Prince Charles was our past President and when he handed the office over to me, he had another fellow to do it because it was too heavy. Prince Philip is our permanent twelfth man – he never goes in – he never comes out!

Women's Cricket

Abroad there are, it seems to me, more female supporters in the game of cricket than there are in Britain, especially in Australia. There they have a great number of lady stands where men are only allowed if they are accompanied by a female member. You don't see this often in England, although there is one at Trent Bridge and one at Worcester. It is certainly something to be encouraged because once ladies are introduced to the mystique of cricket it's as enjoyable as a new hair do.

All dressing-room attendants should be female and should not be able to say 'No' in five languages.

I can't talk much about women's cricket because I must admit I have never played against a women's side in my life. I have spoken to Rachel Heyhoe-Flint, who is a great friend of mine. A very straight-talking lady indeed. She said she knows that women could never come up to the standard of men in the game, and whenever they do play against men cricketers, the men have to take it that little bit easier. Apparently there have been one or two occasions when the men bowlers have got a little upset and the odd lady cricketer has more than held her own. One has to be very careful when playing against ladies with a hard ball as you may hit them in certain parts of their anatomy and that would never do. I am told that a lady's body is different and more sensitive than that of a man. I was pleased to see lady cricketers finally received when it was agreed that they could play in a Test match at Lord's. Quite a few people went along to watch that game. Believe me, I'm all for anything like that which helps to foster cricket and its relationships at all levels. Ladies tour extensively but they have to rely very much on sponsorship, which is not easy for them to obtain. There is room for ladies cricket in the set up, let's face it, we are always looking for entertainment and I feel sure that ladies on the cricket field can give some very fine performances!

The most important thing for a man to do when playing cricket is to wear a box. But what about women cricketers, what do they wear? I am told that they wear something known as a man-hole cover, and I am one of the few people who can actually raise a man-hole cover — with a lot of effort of course.

I think there should be an England male team playing an England female team and they should only have one dressing-room and whoever wants to go out, can.

Masseurs

I was a very lucky man – in 20 years of cricket I never had the misfortune to pull a muscle so I can't talk very much about them. I have seen people with pulled muscles and believe me they can be nasty, especially if they tear and bleed. You can see the blackness where the blood has run from the tear. I'm told that it is very painful.

Most of the masseurs I came across in first class cricket were a joke. A lot of them were just people who at best could give you a rub. When it comes down to the nitty gritty, the expertise of knowing exactly what has happened when a player is injured, this can only be provided by a doctor or someone who is completely qualified. There were a lot of masseurs in my time who, if they had taken exams, would have failed miserably. Sometimes I have thought some masseurs must think the players are cattle and not human beings, the way they treat them. I know that if ever I felt that there was something wrong with me I would never consult the Yorkshire masseurs. I would always go and see my doctor first and find out really what the trouble was. That would be my advice to all young players if not quite sure of the qualifications of the man in the white coat in the dressing-room. Things are changing a lot now. Pavilions have treatment facilities and qualified masseurs. But in my day, if you wanted anything doing, it was a case of just lying on the rough wooden table in the middle of the dressing-room to get rubbed down appropriately. I have even seen masseurs wanting to give injections to the lads and I have told them, 'Not on your Nellie'.

It was Charlie Harris of Nottinghamshire who dived at short leg to take a catch and landed on the point of his shoulder. Charlie had to be helped from the field in dire pain, he was eventually taken to the hospital and on to the second floor. Whilst they were taking his shirt off he was humming and hawing and growning in pain. The doctor diagnosed a dislocation, but assured Charlie that he would soon put it back. With that he got a hold of Charlie's arm, wrenched it round and slotted it straight back into place. The scream was heard all over the hospital. A nurse came in and said, 'Mr Harris, I watch Nottinghamshire play cricket and I always thought you to be a very tough man, but here you are having your shoulder put back in and the scream is heard all over the hospital. There is a little girl next door, 21-years-of-age – for the first time in her life she has given birth to twins and we never had any noise like that from her.' 'No', Charlie said, 'but you try putting the buggers back'.

Lots of bowlers, though I was never one, used to like their thighs and the backs of their hamstrings given a good rub and warm up by the heat lamp before they went onto the field. I never did this kind of thing, I used to find that a few exercises was enough. I'd knock my legs about myself. If you relax and put your leg up on a bench you can move the hamstring about quite easily. The same applies with the calf muscle, to loosen it I used to do what is called, pulling the muscle off the bone, or something similar. I always had a quick little run to the wicket, then a practice run up, before I started to bowl. Then for the first over I wouldn't try to bowl as quickly as I possibly could, and sometimes not even in the second over unless I felt right. Usually by the third over everything was working. I'd warmed myself, loosened and got in rhythm. Only then did I start bowling quicker and looked to the job in hand.

Of the many masseurs, one comes to mind in my cricketing times, Bright Heyhirst. A nice little man who liked to smoke his pipe, he was definitely a character. Mind you he would only rub the players he liked. You could be sure he would always be ready to see what time you came into the hotel. So you had to be very careful because he would tell the

52

down. The only troubles I really had were blisters underneath my left foot, the front foot. This used to happen if my bootlace had worked loose and with constantly banging my left foot down on the ground at point of delivery, my foot pushed up against the toe of the boot. The sock would probably roll up underneath as well and I wouldn't notice it until it was too late. I used to get blisters under my foot and some of them would be as big as an old penny. They were really the only injuries I ever had. You have to look at the make-up of some people to see if they are really athletic enough by the way they run. After all, the human body was not built for the twisting, throwing and abuse it gets in the game of cricket when bowling.

Once when one of our players cut his toe badly on the dressing-room floor, he went looking for the masseur. Eventually he found him with a little stall at the end of the pavilion selling small miniature cricket bats that he had carved out of wood, about three inches long. He got us all to sign them and was selling them at ten shillings apiece. That wasn't Bright Heyhirst, that was another gentleman who didn't stay with us too long.

The equipment used by cricket masseurs is generally less good than that for other sports, except perhaps on the big Test grounds, where you do find good equipment and proper people to use it. There are, however, many grounds where the facilities to get dressed or undressed to play the game are completely inadequate. You cannot expect equipment on these unless it has been bundled into a car. Usually it's to the nearest hospital as quick as possible. Lotions and sprays, I also feel, can be a little dangerous. I remember years ago, I think it was at Scarborough Festival, when that great cricketer and great friend of ours Colin Milburn sprayed his bottom. When he warmed up you could hear him jumping about, shouting and squealing. I will never forget the sight of him sitting completely naked with his backside in the sink and his feet dangling over the edge, breathing sighs of relief!

I laugh when I tell the story but it also happened to me. Bright Heyhirst had his own liniment which he carried in a jar. Believe me it was the hottest bloody stuff that has ever been invented. I remember my back being a little stiff at the base and asking Bright to let me put some of his ointment on it. We were playing at Sheffield at the time. I'm not kidding you, my back was burned scarlet red. It looked as if I had been badly sunburned. Some of it ran right down and into my backside and I can tell you that I then did some of the quickest bowling that I have ever produced in my life! I know I finished up at Sheffield with my shirt hanging out running down the hill trying to get a draught to keep me cool.

captain or the committee when he got back about your behaviour. One night in London, a Monday night, whilst we were playing at The Oval there was a mess up in the bookings. I went out with three of the other players to have a meal and then on to the cinema. We went back to the hotel and had a couple of beers and were in bed just before midnight. The next morning I was in the dressing-room, and having had a hard bowl the afternoon before and feeling a little stiff, I thought for a change I would have a little bit of heat treatment and possibly a quick rub down. Bright said, 'Anyone who can come in after half-past four in the morning and expect to bowl fast doesn't need a rub down'. So when I enquired what he meant he told me that he had waited up for us until after half-past four and I hadn't returned to the hotel. The captain of the side said, 'Is that true, Freddie?' So I said, 'No, I was in bed last night before twelve o'clock', and Bright Heyhirst called me a liar. So I asked the other three players who were with me and they all agreed and said, 'Yes, we were in bed before twelve o'clock, skipper'. Whereupon the captain asked Bright where he was staying and he said, 'At the Denmark'. 'Well there's no wonder you sat up until half-past bloody four with the night porter', said the captain. 'These lads are staying at Snows Hotel up the road.'

I think I was a very fortunate man, I rarely broke

Who's for the Beer?

There is nothing wrong with sportsmen having a drink, I reckon, as long as it is in moderation. For instance, fast bowlers like myself have probably bowled 25 to 30 overs by the end of a hot day. Some sort of fluid must go back into the body to maintain the balance. If not, it would become completely dehydrated. Beer doesn't affect the players' weight because they run around all day in the hot sun, if lucky, and their bodies will sweat it out. Abroad, on many occasions, you have to take salt tablets, and I mean big salt tablets. I couldn't take them because they used to make me sick. So I used to have my salt on food, and a lot of it. Some players drink

rather a large amount of alcohol – beer, gin and tonic, whisky and the like, and it's up to the individual to know when he has had enough. Having a drink also eases tension and, in fact, the cricketer is more likely to sweat it out of his body than an ordinary person who sits in the crowd. Even so, I would never encourage young men to take alcohol, I would discourage them. These days I play cricket quite often against public schools and they have their own bars installed for the boys and the visiting teams, although I must point out that the lads who drink are mostly over eighteen. Drink has sometimes got the better of the crowds. It is a well known fact that when the wags start shouting the beers are taking effect. You can set the clock by it sometimes. It usually starts just after tea about twenty minutes to five, when the beer and the sun mixture is starting to take effect. If they heard some of the things they say on tape recordings afterwards,

I'm sure they would be thoroughly ashamed of themselves. Sometimes it is more than voices and abuse that is thrown. I have been through two riots in the West Indies, when bottles have whistled past my head.

Whatever you say about the game of cricket one thing is certain and that is that it is a very big social game. There are many social rounds in Britain and abroad which cricket celebrities are expected to attend. At the end of the season most county sides have a party on the last night and believe me, some of these are bloody hilarious. It is a tradition in cricket that when the players come off the field drinks are served for them in the dressing-room. Many is the time I have seen the twelfth man make a few journeys to the bar for his tray of ten pints, orange juice, and a gin and tonic for the captain, if he was an amateur. There is one famous story about a Yorkshire cricketer before the turn of the century, who was sent from the field for drinking, never to play for Yorkshire again. How true it is I don't know. Apparently he marked his run up out and then set off to bowl and bowled at the side-screen!

When you go abroad on tour for seven months, you can guarantee that there will be definitely at least three to four cocktail parties a week, plus private parties on a Saturday evening. These do not include the official dinners you are expected to attend. So drink and food is always there available in front of you. Many times abroad I have actually seen glasses of beer brought on to the field for players who have requested it during the hours of play. Once I saw a Scotch and water brought out. I do remember hearing about two famous Australian fast bowlers who, in aid of an all out effort to try and win a match, actually had whisky and burnt brown sugar brought out to them. I must add that there was little point in it because England still won that certain Test match at Sydney.

One way to avoid too much drinking on tour is to play golf. A lot of players are very keen golfers, none probably more keen than Brian Close who can play right- or left-handed. Brian's temperament sometimes lets him down and he has been known in some golfing circles as a club thrower. A club can go whistling anywhere, once he has played a bad shot. He threw a club so hard once, it got fast in a tree. He threw another to try and knock it down and finished climbing up the tree to get both clubs out. Another time he threw a club and lost it in the long grass. I think the best golfing story I have heard about Brian was told to me by a great mate of his and mine called Don Mosey. Closey once played a terrible shot when playing a foursome with Don. He threw the trolley, the bag, the clubs, the whole lot straight into the middle of the lake and stormed off muttering about not wanting to

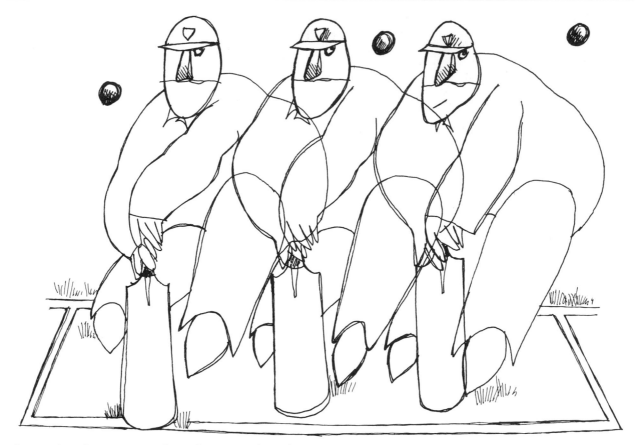

play again. The rest carried on playing without him and passed the lake on their way back playing the next hole, only to find Closey, trousers rolled up to his knees in the middle of the water retrieving the golf bag. Don Mosey said to him, 'I thought you were never going to play golf again?' Closey replied, 'I'm bloody well not, but I've got to get at my golf bag, my car keys are in it'.

I remember Ossie Wheatley and Colin Ingleby-Mackenzie tossing up at Bournemouth in dinner jackets, having returned from a function in London just before a match was due to start. At least that isn't quite as bad as a story of a player who was three sheets to the wind and was forced to bat because his side needed two to win. When he got to the wicket he tried unsuccessfully to hit the first five balls. When the wicket keeper asked him what the matter was, he said that he was so Harry Liszt that he could see three balls. So the keeper suggested that he hit the middle one. The sixth ball came down and the drunken batsman took a large wild swing, missed the ball again, and the keeper said, 'I told you to hit the middle one'. The drunk replied, 'Yes, but you didn't tell me which bat to hit it with'.

A fellow walked into a pub one day with a dog on a lead and the landlord approached him and said,

'If I were you I would take that dog out of here.' 'Why?' said the man, 'it is doing no harm, it's gentle and very quiet.' 'Yes', the landlord said, 'but there is another dog in the pub and this dog is a very vicious one, it fights any dog it sees no matter how big the other dog is or how ferocious. As a matter of fact, it's the champion around here and it's been known on at least four other occasions to kill the dog it's fighting. We have a lot of trouble, so if you would take my advice you would walk you dog home.' The fellow said, 'No thank you, I don't think I've got to worry.' Anyway his dog sat very quietly on the lead whilst the other more ferocious one was in a corner growling and showing its teeth. Suddenly it was up and flew at the quiet one and this quiet one turned round and grabbed the champion killer by the neck. It dragged it around the floor and around the bar, and smashed it against the wall – nobody could stop them. People were jumping on chairs and tables to get out of the way. The quiet dog eventually killed the champion dog and the landlord, scratching his head, said, 'I just don't believe it, I don't believe it. What sort of dog is that you've got there?' The man said, 'I don't know. My brother, as you know, plays international cricket and he brought this thing back from South Africa. I just shaved off its mane.'

The Laws of Cricket

The laws are set by the ICC, they are then given out to the different countries and their associations to implement. Some laws, however, are introduced by the home governing body. This is something else that has always amazed me. Year after year new laws have been brought out with little or no consultation with the players currently in the game. Perhaps they thought we would know what we were talking about and ruin the sequence. Way back in 1963 we ran into a farce, when the West Indies came to this country with two fast bowlers called Wesley Hall and Charlie Griffiths. Both refused to play under the front-foot rule. Now when I talk about the front-foot rule as it was then, the whole of the front foot had to be behind the front line. I found this rule difficult anyway but when we could please ourselves whether or not we used it in Tests or representative matches against the West Indies,

it was bloody hard. I felt like putting my foot where it would really count. The umpires helped as much as they could. I remember asking the late Syd Buller if he would let me know if it got too close to the bowling line. He said, 'Yes, Fred, I'll call you'. The introduction of the laws about front foot, dragging, the return crease, keep off the wicket, and suchlike, brought about a new type of bowler, one with a degree. Many batsmen thought that bowlers would be in short supply because of the number of tests they had to pass before they could qualify. In the end it comes down to the players out on the square who have to try and make the rules work. Sometimes for some players it is very difficult. This is where I think a better liaison between the players and the TCCB could lead to better cricket and a better relationship which I found at times throughout my career very sadly missing.

In fact, at one time the changes in laws were coming in so thick and fast that at a game between Yorkshire and Sussex at Bradford Park Avenue I saw an ex-England bowler turned umpire called Bill Copson, who has unfortunately now passed on, reach into his pocket and take out a book of rules on the game of cricket, to see which rule a certain situation came under.

What a position to find yourself in, in front of a huge crowd. In fact it happened when Yorkshire were playing Sussex. We had Sussex eight wickets down and I was bowling. With the last ball of my over I clean bowled one of their players, which left them with nine wickets down and two minutes to go. John Snow, the England bowler batting number eleven for Sussex, came down the steps of the pavilion and actually reached the playing square itself. The umpire at square leg had put the stump back, the bails on and was standing waiting. The Sussex player at the other end said to the umpire, 'I can see it's not full time yet but John Snow isn't taking strike, I am. Does the umpire have to walk from square leg to the wicket after John has arrived, or is he alright standing there already?' The umpires had to get together in the middle of the square and consult the rule books. They eventually took the bails off and left the field still in bewilderment. At one time it was thought that Yorkshire were going to phone Lord's to ask the ruling, but there wouldn't have been time to get a ruling before play or playing time ended because it was over 200 miles to London!

The laws of the game as I see it are wrong and they haven't been changed for at least half an hour. If a batsmen gets into the nineties, I think the bowler should be allowed on his last ball to bowl down a hand-grenade. If the batsman hits it, he's out well and truly. If he misses it the wicket keeper is out, and if the wicket keeper misses it the crowd is out. I think the size of stumps is correct but there should be more of them. I think there should be three with two bails on the top of those and no hole in the middle. The wicket keeper should wear gloves because the ball is hard and the batsmen should be allowed to wear pads on his legs.

I would like to see a change in the lbw rule, I have always thought how stupid and silly it is when a bowler such as myself can bowl a couple of inches outside the leg stump, bowl an away swinger which would swing the ball back definitely hitting middle or middle and off, and get a 'not out' decision. Yet somebody these days can bowl nine inches to a foot outside the off-stump and the batsman can be given out lbw because in the opinion of the umpire the ball would have hit the stumps. This leads to bad play. When you talk to the old players they all say, 'people don't play off the back foot today like they used to do'. The reason is obvious, it is the lbw rule. That is why they cannot bloody well play off the back foot now, they have got to try to get onto the front foot with the bat and pad to protect themselves, which creates defensive batting. If they could get onto the back foot, knowing full well that the bowler pitching outside the off-stump would not get a decision if the ball nipped back, they could play many more and freer shots.

Something should be done about the running on the pitch law. A bowler should be able to bowl wicket to wicket, and to do that he should be able to get very close to the stumps. I get on to young bowlers about this telling them that they have got to get close to the stumps if they are to bowl the best line, and quite rightly they tell me to bugger off as they can't get close to the stumps because they are afraid of running on the wicket – for which, of course, these days a bowler can be taken off. Not being able to bowl again in that innings is something he obviously can't afford. So what we get is bowlers bowling wide, and delivering wide of the crease does no more than to bring in defensive inswing bowling. We very rarely see outswing bowlers these days and let's face it the game of cricket, whether you are batting or bowling, is supposed to be a sideways-on game, and that is what creates outswing bowling. Today it is becoming very chest on, whether you are batting or bowling, which can only be bad for the technique of the game.

The 100 overs rule is a very bad rule to my way of thinking because 100 overs in the first innings is mad. I would only just begin to warm up by that number. I think it is detrimental to cricket because what we find is one, two, three or four batsmen taking up say, 75 to 90 overs, then the youngsters coming in who want to make the grade are suddenly faced with 10 overs to cement their future. It is not a case of being able to get their heads down and try to plan an innings and try to play themselves into the side, they have got to throw the bat for bonus points, they are hitting across the line and their feet are in the wrong positions. It must be a nightmare for kids in the middle order batting, trying to make their way into first class cricket. Then you can guess what happens – we come right back to the short-sighted committee men who read the paper the next day, see where so-and-so has got five, what's-his-name has got seven and another player nine, and not realising the circumstances the young men have had to play under, recommend changes. Suddenly a boy is dropped because he is not producing the goods and the confidence of the kid is shattered. We have probably lost, once again, a promising young player. We should protect our middle order batsmen and give them a chance to play.

Another rule I would definitely change is the one governing overs in an hour. This is absolutely ridiculous. If a captain has two fast bowlers bowling at the same time and they are taking wickets he is not going to want to take them off. This could happen in five or six matches in a month and now that the fine is monthly and not yearly it is going to make matters very difficult for him. It is a very silly rule indeed. I always reckoned that when Brian Statham and I were bowling in our prime in Test matches, or representative matches, we were managing sixteen overs to the hour, that's if we were going well. If we were getting wickets as well, there was no way we would have got sixteen overs in an hour.

No balls – now this is something that has always interested me, being a quick bowler. I have played under so many stupid rules that the mind boggles. At one time we had a disc for the drag. Then we had to drop with our front foot behind the front line. Then we could cut the front line and this we can still do. At least the law makers have tried to keep this last law going for some years. I see many no balls bowled today that are not called because the bowler's back foot is outside the return crease. You can't blame the poor old umpire for this because he can only watch one foot at a time. He can't look at the back foot and the front foot, try to see where the ball pitches, and try to give a decision as well.

Most bowlers bowl wides. I have bowled a few. Even the great Brian Statham, who was one of the most accurate fast bowlers in the history of the game, bowled wides. Sometimes, in humid conditions, if you happened to be bowling just a little wide of the off-stump and the ball really swings away, third slip could stop it. Sometimes there is nothing the bowler can do about the swing. The ball sets off somewhere on line and ends up going late, perhaps as much as a yard wide. Then there are the interpretations of a wide delivery. For example, in the one-day Prudential Test matches, if a bouncer is bowled and in the opinion of the umpire it is too high, it is a wide. In one-day cricket if a couple of deliveries go down the leg side and the batsman doesn't play at them, they are given as wides. Yet sometimes you see a ball a yard outside the off-stump but no wide is given. It's another law that in my opinion wants sorting out once and for all.

In general, the laws are not too bad. Although I believe quite a few could be changed for the betterment of the game. Things like the restriction of fielders behind square. Let's face it, we want to be encouraging slow bowlers at the present moment, not discouraging them. The off-spinner with this law, bowling on a turning wicket, can no longer have two short legs behind the wicket, unless he does away with his fine leg, which is an important position for him. The batsman playing against the ball turning in, is obviously going to play the sweep shot. So the bowler should be allowed more than two behind to encourage the batsmen to play him there. He cannot attack that line without fielders on the leg side, so if he can't he will most likely end up bowling flat – something we are trying to discourage. At one time we used to have only five men allowed on the on-side. This was also a bad rule because once again it limited the off-spin bowler. He had to try and attack the off-stump with a turning ball and the best place to hit the turning ball as we are always taught, is with the spin. So the batsman would be hitting on the on-side.

I have never seen anyone's cap drop on the wicket for them to be given out. I have seen some near misses but I have never seen it happen. A lot of people think that it is a bad rule, but I don't think so. If a bowler has been able to bowl quick enough

to make a batsman jerk his head out of the way and the cap has dropped onto the wicket, it is only just reward for the bowler.

I have seen many people hit their wickets. Unfortunately, that is how I broke the world record at Christchurch in 1963 when I passed Brian Statham's 242 wickets. Barry Sinclair playing back, hit his wicket in the most unfortunate way. I always think it is a terrible method of getting out but it is the law of the game. I suppose if a bowler can force a batsman so far back, he should be rewarded with the wicket.

I have never seen anyone given out hitting a ball twice. I don't think anyone would attempt to do it except in unusual circumstances. If the ball they have played is running back onto their wicket, then of course they are within the law to do it. The law only applies if it is deliberate and you are attempting to run after hitting it the second time.

Superstitions

In cricket we have a funny thing about superstitions of the scoreboard. For some unknown reason 111 is known in the world of cricket as Nelson. When I once asked a person how it came about, that 111 should be known as Nelson, he said that it came from the Battle of Trafalgar, where Nelson died, because after he had been shot, he finished up with one arm, one eye and one ambition! The Australians don't like to see 87 on the board, so I enquired about that. They said because it was thirteen short of a hundred. You would be amazed how many wickets fall at 87 in Australia, as in England you would be surprised how many wickets fall at the dreaded Nelson. I have seen cricketers when 111 has been on the board sit with their fingers crossed and their legs crossed until it's got to 112, that's how superstitious some of us can be!

Betting

County cricket for many years has frowned on the idea of bookmakers on cricket grounds or even gambling coming into the game. The man who has had a lot to do with its revival and subsequent move back onto the cricket grounds of England is my old sparring partner, Godfrey Evans. He has done this in spite of the fact that I told him that the

only way to back a horse is into shafts. There are betting tents now available where people can have a flutter on the horses if they have the mind to. Or if they have a crystal ball they can have a bet on the actual day's play of cricket, who will get the most wickets, who will get the highest score or who will win the match. In fact if there is any chance to it you can bet on it. Some supporters think that this is a bad thing but really it is only a resurrection of something that was taking place quite happily over 200 years ago, and if gambling is going to exist in our society why not in cricket?'

Streakers

Of course during modern times and the permissive society that we have found ourselves living in, it was inevitable that sometime during a Test match we would have a streaker, and this did happen in a Test match at Lord's, England v Australia. At the time John Arlott was doing the commentary and without his voice faltering he went through a full description of the event, a marvellous piece of broadcasting. It's funny, we get thousands of letters on our radio Test match special, and it is a fact that we only ever got one letter concerning the streaker. It was from some dear old lady enquiring about the dimensions of the policeman's hat that was used to cover up the private parts as they took the streaker out of the ground!

There have been streakers every-where but only one famous one at Lord's, a male streaker. The police-man only had and needed one helmet, but what if a woman streaker appeared? I mean are there policemen with three helmets? I did know of a female streaker out in Australia at a place called Tamarama. She ran across the field but she didn't actually strip off, she wore black fur boots, black fur gloves and did a fantastic impression of the five of spades, which was a little difficult because she was blonde. As she ran away from the police she looked like Kojak with a deep frown.

THE FORCE BE WITH ME

The Game off the Field

THE ORDER AND DISORDER OF THINGS IN THE WORLD OF CRICKET'S ADMINISTRATORS

The ICC

The ICC sounds more like an Italian ice cream to me.

In the beginning there is the ICC, the International Cricket Council. This is the body that controls cricket throughout the world. I can honestly admit that I do not know who the members of the ICC are. I see them as the faceless wonders. The mafia of cricket. It might surprise you to learn that I have never knowingly met the people who run the game, but that is what cricket is – no one ever knowing who's who, does what or with which or to whom. I did come across one who was a right bore, who through money, became a part of the game. As far as I know that man still represents the United States of America, which when you think about it would possibly be the best role for him, because the United States of America does not play international cricket. Perhaps he was the one to introduce the front-foot law. I have always wanted to give my front foot to the person who did that.

KEEP POLITICS OUT OF SPORT SPORTS MINIZTER!

One of the most delicate subjects that the ICC has had to deal with is the outlawing of South Africa as a cricketing nation. For me politics and cricket are as wide apart as the banks of the Amazon and should be kept that way. I can tell you that the South African cricketers are not worried about the colour of a man's skin. All they want to do is play the game. We hear, though how true one can never tell, that there are only two or three countries in the world of cricket who object to playing against South Africa. This is the result of politics in the game where once again we seem to have minorities ruling majorities. Most players I talk to around the world believe it to be one of the greatest shames in cricket that South Africa is no longer able to play at Test level, because they became a cricketing nation to reckon with. When

you think of names like Pollock, both Peter and Graeme, Graeme being possibly one of the greatest left-hand batsman of all time, and of Eddie Barlow, Mike Procter, Barry Richards and other like these wonderful players, you wonder why the world has been denied the opportunity of enjoying them just because a few obstinate men prefer it that way. Sometimes cricket makes me bloody miserable.

I see no reason why we shouldn't play cricket in South Africa, nor can I see any reason why we shouldn't have the South African players here. It's like saying we can't play Iceland because in Iceland they kill whales and there is a great conservation thing about whales. I love whales, I married one, I should know. I am sure that if this subject was put to the country in referendum form you would find that the majority of people would want to see South Africans play. After all, it is only entertainment not war. Barry Richards and Mike Procter have been playing in this country for some time and we have taken them to heart. They don't change in different dressing-rooms from their coloured colleagues as the English gentlemen used to in the amateur and professional days. If we want to endorse the political scene in sport, it seems a bit strange to me that we play football against Russia, Poland and Czechoslovakia. All are communist countries and their restrictions on human rights are just as strong as the South Africans. If we want to do the job properly let's give America back to the Indians, South America back to the Incas, Australia to the Aborigines and England to the Cornish and give up sport altogether.

It is sad that this position today prevails but one good thing came out of the problem and from South Africa. That's Basil D'Oliveira, who came and, one could only say, conquered, because he played for England. Basil D'Oliveira to me became more English than a lot of English people and is one of the most likeable characters that I have met in my cricketing career.

The biggest problem the ICC have had to face since the war is the start of what has now been called the Kerry Packer Circus. When this came to a head in 1977 it was no surprise to me. A bigger

surprise was the fact that the ICC had not been confronted much earlier with a similar problem. People ask me if I would have joined the Kerry Packer circus at the age of 35 when they dropped me from Test cricket without any explanation. My answer is simple – I feel sure that my wife and children would have come first and the type of money that Mr Packer is offering would have tempted me to play for his Circus without hesitation. Blind loyalty is one thing but it doesn't pay for the victuals. When I hear the talk of player loyalty I wonder why many county clubs find little use for the word when they consider a player's future with them.

There is an Indian who is going to take over the world of cricket called Curry Packy.

If cricket doesn't pull itself together and shake itself out of the deep Rip Van Winkle sleep that it finds itself in, what Mr Packer is doing is definitely going to take hold. Someone is going to make commercial cricket work. Our younger players are far more commercially-minded than they were in my day, and they are looking forward to making the right sort of money to enable them to retire comfortably. A lot of people in the hierarchy seem to

think that cricketers make a fortune during their playing days, but believe me this is not true. Cricketers have two old ages, the normal one and the first one when they are too old to play cricket. I'm all for the Packer type of set up if it is going to bring cricket more money, particularly for the players. It certainly started things happening. At the end of last season a private individual by the name of David Evans, found a company willing to put up a million pounds over five years. It's strange it needed something like the Kerry Packer Circus to stimulate that type of interest. Even so, I still think it's a bad deal, it should have been that amount on a yearly basis.

The trouble at the moment for a cricketer, is that to make money he has got to work seven-and-a-half days a week, so I have no objection to Kerry Packer coming into the game and changing it around. You have got to have progress and that often means change. I'm for him. I don't think he has gone about it in the right way, but that's my opinion. The point is that in his opinion he's gone about it the right way and I wish him all success. I think what he has done has been beneficial to the game already because in this country we do two things, we stand still or we go back. He has gone a step forward and we have all gone 'Jesus Christ'.

I would like to see the Americans enter the cricket world in a big way. I remember playing at the Sir Aubrey Smith Bowl in Hollywood. Cricket was pioneered there by that great man, who played for Sussex and became a film star. I was surprised at the interest and the amount of cricket that is played. In fact I met many Americans who took their holidays to coincide with the Test matches being played in the West Indies.

I remember Fred Trueman when he was President of America.

Only last year a match was played in America and that great all-rounder Sir Garfield Sobers was the star. It was promoted in a baseball or football ground, and they had a staggering crowd. The gate money received was something in the region of $50,000. It gives you some idea of how cricket can and should be promoted, not only in the United States but in Europe and the rest of the world. Some counties don't take that amount of money at the gate in five years let alone one match.

Canadians have played cricket as far as we know since 1827 and although the standard is pretty good, to improve they should be playing on turf wickets and not on matting. The most beautiful ground I have ever seen is in Canada, in Vancouver. Many countries throughout the world play cricket now and I would like to feel that the ICC was actively encouraging them to improve their standards. They could even begin with Canada, then more teams could qualify for the first league making the future of the game more secure.

The amazing thing about cricket is that it never fails to fascinate the people who initially only take a passing interest and it usually forces them to take up the game seriously. It is now on the up and up all over Europe as a result of being played by the British Services and consuls who are scattered all over that continent. I played cricket in Germany

HOLLYWOOD CRICKET CLUB

when I was in the RAF way back in the 1950s and Germans are very, very keen. I think this is where the ICC could do a good job by sending teams out there made up of older players with a sprinkling of youth to give the youngsters some idea of what it's like to go abroad. It would also teach the same youngsters the basic technical points that the older players know so well. The standard of these players would rub off within the countries that were visited and the overall upgrading would certainly be to the game's advantage at international level. The only place that might frighten me to play cricket would be, of course, Holland where they are very enthusiastic. I was very happy to accept a Yorkshire county cap and very delighted to accept an England cap but I wonder what they would award you in Holland?

The Irish of course love cricket. I remember once when an England team played over there our captain said to the Irish captain, 'where's your bowler? He replied, 'We only wear caps here.'

Aus der Gemeinsamkeit der faschistischen und der nationalsozialistischen Revolution ist heute eine Gemeinsamkeit nicht nur der Ansichten, sondern auch des Handelns gekommen. Dies ist aber ein Glück in einer

The TCCB

There are so many committees and bodies that the mind boggles at where they come from and what they do. The TCCB, the Test and County Cricket Board, is the committee that governs and runs the game of cricket at both county and international level. The TCCB is a committee which in the main is made up of representatives from each of the first class counties, usually the chairman and the secretary. Their job is to administer the first class game. Once again I think this is where the game of cricket sometimes falls down. I feel sure that they are trying to do their best because most of them, when you really get down to it, are like ourselves — passionately in love with the game and wanting to see it progress. But we do tend to get people who still live the dark past and do not realise that the game of cricket, like any other sport, is now a commercial proposition. We find a lot of people sitting on these county committees simply because they have the time to spare to try to do the job. It is unfortunate that we do not engage active qualified men whose minds live in this present era and who use their business sense to do a good job.

This type of man is able to bring more money into the game and administer it in a modern way, which I feel is so badly needed. I don't think for one minute that the people who represent the TCCB have enough time to make their decisions, particularly when you find some are travelling from as far as two or three hundred miles to Lord's for meetings. It has been said by some chairmen in the north of England that they would like to move the TCCB out of Lord's into the centre of the country to make it easier to get to, then they could possibly spend a little more time getting the rules and administration right and less time in second class train compartments.

I have been told that the greatest humour comes out of the game of cricket and that is why Des O'Connor has never played. You all remember Des, short for desperate. Des was an athlete, he has what is known as athlete's voice — when you hear him sing you want to run.

County Cricket

It is the county cricket committees who have to put into action the recommendations, suggestions or the rules that the TCCB pass on to them. This is where I think the difficult part starts because they have to be worked into the established structure of a county club. Now talking about county cricket, the county I know most about is of course the one I played for, Yorkshire. When I sit and think back how one man could take a committee by the throat and be the be-all and end-all of power, I worry. I found that for the committee, at times, there was only one side to a story and that was theirs. Some of the professional players were always in some sort of trouble or other and usually the thing that hurt them most was that committee men, who had been amateur players, obviously did not know how the professional cricketer worked or thought. As I have said on many occasions when in a committee room, if I had committed murder and was in court, at least I would be able to tell my side of the story. In my day the professional side of the story was non-existent, and even if a pro was allowed to tell it he would be wasting his breath, because the conclusions would have been reached most likely before he went in for the hearing.

County Committees

I don't know about other county clubs, but in Yorkshire people are put forward in different areas to serve on the committee. I believe it has just over 40 members. What I do find is that the people who come from these different areas are the popular sort of figures who know everybody, like solicitors, barristers and accountants. They stand because they would like to be a member of a cricket committee. They love the game dearly but often, unfortunately, they know very little about it. This is where I think the grass roots of certain of the troubles in the game really start. One thing I do know is that all committee members have to learn the ritual game of who can be sacked this year – it's played about August every year behind closed doors.

My favourite game the wife won't let me play any more, so the next loved is cricket.

STAND BACK, I'M
AN ESTATE AGENT

We want people who know something about the game. I say we ought to have older players particularly on the selection committee. They usually know a good player when they see one. If there is a finance committee, then yes, we need good businessmen and accountants to run the job properly and to make money. We need people in the property world to sit on ground committees to provide better facilities for the spectators and members alike. I know a barrister on a ground committee and probably the only grass he knows about is outside his house, and somebody else cuts that for him. We have got to try and get a proper balance to our committees. We need to cut them down in size, with members who are cricketers who have played the game and recognise good cricketers when they see them; financial men who understand the business world and how to make money for the game; property men who know about buildings, and any other experts where and when required. We shouldn't need charity fund raisers who are experts in football pools. If ICI wanted a chemist they would not employ a bricklayer to do the job, and vice versa.

There are far too many people just wanting the glory of wearing a committee tie or being a member of that body. On one occasion I remember I had just played in a Test match at Lord's and was playing for my county at Bradford and I had had a fairly good morning with three or four wickets under my belt before lunch and was sitting in the dressing-room having just taken my shirt off. One of the committee men came in and peered around the room. Eventually he came up towards me and I thought 'this fellow is going to tread all over me if he gets any closer', when suddenly he looked down his nose something like four inches from mine and said 'It's Freddie isn't it?' and I said, 'yes, yes'. 'Ah! how nice to see you', he said, 'I have been wanting to meet you'. It suddenly struck me that from four inches away he didn't know me from Adam and yet he was on the selection committee making decisions on whether or not I played! Of course they have always done things in a different way in Yorkshire.

I have heard of another instance at another county, when the committee met to talk about the termination of a player's contract. Two of the committee members sacked the wrong player because they neither knew him by name nor by sight. I could imagine how they felt. When things like this happen there is no wonder the professional cricketers become agitated. I can imagine such a thing happening at ICI with so many employees, but less than 20 men are employed by county cricket clubs.

I remember when I came very close to striking a committee man. It was during a meeting of the players and the committee with sensible talk about the cost of living and more wages to bring them into line, when one committee man had the audacity to say that if you employ labourers, you pay labourers wages. It was only through determined self-control that I didn't knock him into next year. I was disgusted to think a man could sit on the committee and have that attitude – believing that labourers were as badly paid as we were.

I heard a story way back in the thirties from an old mate of mine, a fast bowler called Reg Perks who has since sadly passed away. He remembered playing against the young Leonard Hutton when he made his first century against Worcester at Worcester. It was a big hundred and when Worcester played the return match against Yorkshire in Yorkshire, Len Hutton was not playing. Reg Perks asked one of the committee members the whereabouts of the young Hutton who had made this magnificent hundred at Worcester. He was met with the reply of, 'He's back in t'second team to get his bloody feet on the ground'. Reg Perks said to me, 'When I got eight wickets in a match at Worcester, they gave me a seven year contract.'

The biggest stumbling block I found with the committee was the lack of liaison between the committee room and the dressing-room. Nobody ever seemed to know what was happening. Suddenly we would be told to do something and that was it, we did it. I feel sure the players would enjoy being more concerned with the running of the club because the benefits go both ways, for the player and the committee. After all we are all in the club for the same cause and that is to win the Championship, or any other honours that are going about. When committee men walk into dressing-rooms I see a lot of players absolutely freeze, even light cigarettes being so nervous – I used to light a cigar.

The committee is sub-divided so that, for example, you have a cricket committee, a selection committee, a finance committee, a ground committee, and I do believe that Yorkshire have a finance raising committee! Everything has to be split up for some unknown reason. It's a wonder I didn't find myself bowling in Bradford and Jimmy Binks keeping at Headingly in the same match. Mark you, some said I was that quick.

DIFFERENCES IN THE FINANCE COMMITTEE HAVE ALWAYS BEEN SETTLED WITH A WILKINSON SWORD

A lot of people who want to sit on county committees and enjoy the privileges of exclusivity, by taking their wives and friends to sit in complete comfort, don't pay enough for it. If they wish to enjoy this sort of privacy, where they sit in the no go areas, they should be prepared to pay large sums, or to get off their backsides, get out into their counties and sell sponsorship for home fixtures. Every match should be sponsored to cover completely the players and staff wages – in Yorkshire's case the rentings of the grounds. I think Yorkshire pay, in some cases, £750 or a third of the gate money to the ground on which they play. If they had every match sponsored by either national or local firms, which can be done, it would have an enormous bearing on bringing stability to the club, providing better facilities and making sure that the players are happy. What the cricket public have to realise today is that the younger players are more commercially-minded than we were in our day. They are in it for monetary reward just as much as the enjoyment of playing and when they see the wages being bandied around by factory and shop workers there is no wonder that they get disgruntled. It is always the same old excuse when a cricketer asks for more money, 'I'm sorry we haven't got it', or, 'I'm sorry we can't afford it'. When the players suggest the members fees go up, the committees have fits and are frightened to do anything about it. It has been said to me, 'If that's how you feel, why don't you stand up in front of the members and ask them to pay more money and you will see the uproar that takes place?' Well, if the members think anything about their cricket clubs and their players, I feel quite sure that they would willingly put more money into their clubs. It's a case of having pride in what is yours.

County Members

Members are the life blood of county cricket and though I really appreciate that I still think they do get the game too cheaply. When committees put it to the members that fees should go up, usually an uproar takes place, yet the return offered for membership far exceeds the cost. For instance, if we take the County of Yorkshire where the membership is £12 per year, within that £12 the member gets the five-day Test match at Leeds, which entitles him to go in without paying. A non-member pays £2 per day, so if a Yorkshire member goes for five days he has the equivalent of £10 worth of cricket, leaving him to watch Yorkshire for the rest of the season for only £2, which works out at something like a half-penny per hour. That is what is wrong with the game of cricket – it's too cheap.

But having been indoctrinated over a century to the cheap entertainment, by cost, which cricket allows itself to offer, then they are not going to change their thinking overnight. When you think that a person can be proposed, seconded and accepted to become a member of the MCC with all those wonderful facilities that Lords can offer, for only £20, something has got to be wrong. I feel sure that if the average cricket fan was asked in the region of £40 to become a member of that wonderful Club, double its present charge, it would not be beyond the realistic figure. I know many people who tell me that they would quite willingly pay £50 tomorrow to become a member of the MCC. After all it is the headquarters of cricket and possibly the most exclusive cricket club in the world. The same members will also willingly pay £60 or more a year to be a member of a golf club – it makes me laugh. If cricketers received seven to eight thousand pounds a year apiece they would be more secure and this, I feel sure, would lead to better cricket from them. It could also serve as an inducement to players who think they might be good enough to play county cricket but won't play because of insufficient funds in the game.

I know I am a member of the MCC because I have a tie which tells me so. In Japan it's not called the MCC, it's called the MKK – Marylebone Kami Kasi.

It also makes me laugh when you hear members talking about their committees, saying they're no good, they're not doing this and they're not doing that. In fact they voted them into that position in the first place and are the same people who vote them on again when they come up for re-election. I shouldn't think that they have to change the letter headings very often in Yorkshire.

Freddie Trueman is one of the nicest men that I ever met and one of the greatest cricketers of all time. I know that because he told me.

'PLUM' WARNER BITES YER BOX !

The County Secretary

The hardest job with any county cricket club must be that of the secretary. He is the man who really could be called the go-between. He has to link committee and players, committee and members, link members and players, players and press, committee and press, public and committee. Some secretaries have been known to vanish in that ever-decreasing circle. I certainly feel sorry for them when it is their unfortunate job to have to tell a player that he and his services are no longer required by the club. This must be a very awful moment but he has it to do. I have known hard men break down and cry at that moment. Mark you, the way some counties handle it, it makes you want to cry, they are so insensitive that they consider that two lines on a carbon copy can sometimes be enough.

I have often wondered what ability is required to make a good secretary. Should they need playing experience and know what the game is about? Or, as we see in many county cricket clubs, should they be men who have served their time in the armed services, retired with their pensions and are looking for a job to help subsidise their living? Far be it for me to suggest that cricket would choose people on the cheap, but there have been a lot of the latter. Though why I don't know, because 80 per cent of them have no idea what the game of cricket is all about and they still try to order players about as though they were in uniform. One of the best secretaries in English county cricket, not afraid to speak his mind because he played the game, is Mike Turner of Leicestershire. I can ring Mike in my job now as a journalist and ask him some technical point on any question and he is only too happy to try and give me that answer. You can ring other secretaries and try to get some technical point answered, or some information that might be helpful towards the club and they tend to talk down to you. Another good 'un was an old England colleague and friend of mine, Trevor Bailey, who played for Essex, captained them and was secretary all at the same time. He had a very good idea how his players felt and what they wanted – they never won anything, but seemed to be a happy crowd. He could, by doing this, express their views very expertly to the county committee and then get the views across from both committee to player and player to committee. I think this sort of arrangement works well if you have the right sort of man.

I remember once a player going into a secretary's office to ask for a rise and the secretary said to him, 'Yes, of course, stand on your toes for ten seconds, then bugger off because I'm busy'.

There was a case of a young player who tore the sole off his boot and was returning to the pavilion

RIGHT, MEN, FORWAAAAAARD – PROD!

to change into some pumps when he met the club secretary on his way towards the nets. When asked what he was doing he explained that he had torn the sole off his boot and was changing into his plimsolls. The secretary asked why it was he only had one pair of boots and the player replied, 'The money you pay me here, I can ill afford one pair'. The secretary said, 'Is it as bad as that?' The player replied, 'yes'. So the secretary reached into his back pocket and took out a roll of notes, wrapped in an elastic band which he removed and gave to the player and said, 'Perhaps this will help'.

The late John Nash, who was secretary of the Yorkshire County Cricket Club for 40 years told of a match, Yorkshire v Glamorgan at Harrogate on a Wednesday, Thursday and Friday, when an old-age pensioner went into his office to pay his yearly subs. Mr Nash said, 'Good morning, nice morning'. The old-age pensioner replied, 'Yes, it is a beautiful day'. Mr Nash said 'Isn't is a pity that there are not more people in the ground here at Harrogate on such a beautiful day to see the county cricket being played.' The old-age pensioner said 'Well I wouldn't worry too much about that Mr Nash, I think it will fill up this afternoon.' 'Why do you think that?' 'Because it's half-day at Pateley Bridge', said the pensioner (Pateley Bridge being of course a small village 11 miles from Harrogate with a population of something that might be reaching 1000 !).

The County Championship

Talking about county cricket and the County Championship you really don't have to look hard to see how it has altered. Various types of legislation have been tried. For instance, I played in County Championship cricket when 28 Championship matches were played in a season and on another occasion when 32 Championship matches were played in a season. It all became very unreal. Being a stalwart of the three-day game I believe the County Championship, or the county game, is the one competition which we have to protect at all times because it is the one in which we discover our young players. Through this they are not only learning techniques as batsmen, bowlers and wicket keepers but learning the mental approach so much required to be able to be good enough to play in five-day Test cricket. I emphasise that this is why the County Championship is so important and must be kept alive. We have had it down to 24 matches. I do believe it has been down as low as 20. I think all the big sides must at all times play each other twice and as the Championship sways so much in current years, the top half of the previous year would constitute the top sides. Local rivals should also play each other twice. They don't, and we get county sides disgruntled because strong teams are playing weak teams too often.

I hate to say this but I think county cricket is fading and during the next five to ten years we could well be laying him gently to rest. The Freds tell me that four-day cricket must come soon. Why don't we put all our efforts in to making that work now? When you go to Lord's or any other ground in the country on a County Championship day and see only 300 to 500 people as I did at Edgbaston, it is saddening. Obviously the game is not paying its way and it's not doing its duty by the public or the players. I believe one of the most important things as far as the average sports fan is concerned, the man who actually watches or goes to the ground, is that he wants to be entertained, he wants to see a result at the time that he is there, he doesn't mind if it's a win, a lose or a draw. Of course he minds, but he still wants to see a result. This is one of the benefits of football, a crowd of 50,000 people at a Manchester United match can see a result. They might not see their team win, usually they do, but they might not. In cricket you get abandoned games, two points as against 16 points or something like that — all of which is very confusing.

I think to get a true Championship we must go back to 28 County Championship matches or change the County Championship scene altogether and play 16 four-day matches. If we did change to four-day matches I would like to see them played on Friday, Saturday, Sunday and Monday on covered wickets. If they are properly covered at least you can get straight back onto the pitch once the rain has stopped and there's more chance of a finish. Four-day matches would bring our batsmen into a better mental condition to be able to play in five-day Test matches. I also think it would provide better wickets for batters to bat on. It would give bowlers an attacking incentive knowing they had four days to play and possibly have a chance of a win. But first and foremost it would bring back into the game the slow bowler who I can see, if there is not some action soon, will vanish from the game altogether. I don't mean the flat slow bowler, though on good wickets he would have to throw the ball in the air and force the batsman to play shots to earn his wickets.

I think that the administration is wrong in trying to protect the game for a minority of supporters, and having done that to start crying about not making money. It doesn't give itself the chance to make it in the first place. Ernie and I do an hour-and-a-half show when we go on stage. Now we could make the same money doing 40 minutes, but by giving them a double portion we do ensure full value and a full theatre. I feel sure that if we went from town to town and it got around that we only did half-an-hour or 40 minutes, theatres would not be full and we would have to cut our prices and change our philosophy — it's full value for their money that people want.

HAVE YOU SEEN THE STATE OF THE MARKET? SELL MY DERBYSHIRE!

1	WORCESTERSHIRE (6)
2	Hampshire (1)
3	Northamptonshire (3)
4	Leicestershire (9)
5	Somerset (10)
6	Middlesex (13)
7	Surrey (2)
8	Lancashire (12)
9	Warwickshire (7)
10	Kent (4)
11	Yorkshire (14)
12	Essex (8)
13	Sussex (15)
14	Gloucestershire (5)
15	Nottinghamshire (17)
16	Glamorgan (11)
17	Derbyshire (16)

What we must do in Britain to bring cricket really back to its full glory, is to prepare good hard, fast wickets. Something really must be done about them, they are very bad. To get fast wickets and maintain fast wickets we must be able to pay proper wages to groundsmen to do the job right. It's all right saying that he gets £2000, and lives free in a house, but that is nothing nowadays. The funny thing about wickets is that everybody needs the same type. With a quick wicket the ball comes onto the bat and the batter can play strokes instead of having to punch it out of the mire. A quick wicket encourages fast bowlers to bowl fast and, although I am biased, one of the greatest sights in the world is to see a fast bowler in full flight. And on a quick wicket the slow bowlers, in particular the leg spin bowlers, get a chance. Now if anyone deserves a chance it's leg spin bowlers. I know they give runs away but it's amazing how many wickets they take. I was always taught to believe that the ball leaving the bat was more expensive than the one going the other way. But it's the one that gets people out, and surely that must be the essence of the game as far as bowling is concerned?

In the old days you used to see big scores when leg spinners played and they bowled their 30 or 40 overs, taking 6 for 120. They delighted the crowd because they saw stroke play from the batsman and they saw wickets fall, and at the end of the day a score of anything between 390 and 450. In those days everyone went home happy and had been entertained. At the present moment in the English county cricket scene, with a 100 overs in the first innings, the only things that are being bred are defensive bowling, defensive batting and defensive attitudes – all bad for the game.

Entertainment is the most important word in professional sport. What is not important is a load of old fuddy duddys saying we can't afford to lose the game of county cricket and paying pittances to keep it. You can afford to lose the game of county cricket. It has got to be lost the way it is at the moment. It's a load of you know what. Three days of no money-making – it's a wonder that Grace doesn't turn in his grave. Cricket clubs at present have to make money by holding tombolas, dances and balls (not the umpire's) and all forms of fund raising which have little or no bearing on cricket.

The Gillette Cup

Cricket altered year by year during my career and in 1964 a one-day game entered into the cricket scene, known as the Gillette Cup.

I never shave whilst the Gillette Cup Final is on.

Although a number of Yorkshiremen looked down on it the Gillette Cup for me was dead right. An excellent competition and very much needed, both for bringing money into the game, however

W.G.GRACE FIELDS!

small at the offset, and for offering something different in the way of cricket entertainment. Because of it, competitiveness between the county sides has improved and the introduction of a few minor county teams gives more players the opportunity to play against the first class sides. Of course it is going to suit some teams better than others, Sussex being one of the forerunners in winning the Gillette Cup in the early days on something like three different occasions.

The one-day game didn't suit the Yorkshire set up though because they had been brought up in the diehard tradition of three-day cricket, so in Yorkshire Gillette Cup cricket was treated as a joke – what we called 'tea party cricket' only for south of the Trent! But as it grew in stature, it was realised that money for the counties was to be made, something dear to a Yorkshireman's heart. In true tradition the competition, the first of its kind, had been sold far, far too cheaply. With the advent of television and the satellite and the opportunity to sell around the world I would not have thought one could start talking in terms of sponsorship under

less than £100,000. I do believe that in the early years the competition was sold to Gillette for a paltry £16,000. The obvious incompetence and lack of experience once again showing its ugly head.

I believe in sponsorship. I believe that cricketers should be able to walk out with certain labels on their back like Gillette, Wilkinson or Vauxhall, or whatever, and in my case I would have written on my back 'cobblers' because I would support Freeman, Hardy & Willis. On the front of my shirt would be 'Buy me and stop one', which is a well known family care organisation, and on the green stains of my whites a note from Mothercare, for those mistakes that I have made.

I am sure the committees thought when the Gillette sponsorship was bought that the players would love an additional game to play for the same wage, because only a handful of counties, one I think – and that's a handful – agreed any additional terms. They even grumbled about the expenses. My tax man didn't even do that.

The lads found it a difficult game to play in the beginning not knowing whether to try to hit everything out of sight, push and run or just run for everything. The bowlers didn't know what line to bowl. I am glad to say that eventually everything was sorted out and the Gillette Cup has gone on to be one of the best in England, if not the major, one-day competition. As a matter of interest other countries also run similar competitions.

If I was managing director of a company like Morleys and we sponsored a cricket player and he made a century, I would with my chairman run onto the ground and carry him off ankle high. If he was a woman and she had made a hundred it would be a little bit more embarrassing but a lot more fun. We would run on and never leave the field.

It had to be, that somewhere along the line, Yorkshire would make the Gillette Cup Final and in 1965 after a great tussle with Warwickshire at Birmingham, Yorkshire were in their first final to be played against Surrey. At that time Yorkshire were definitely second favourites, which unbeknown to many people suited us down to the ground. One side that didn't frighten us was definitely Surrey. What a contrast between the two sides. We arrived at Lord's that year and were told that it had rained for 13 days solid and that there was no chance of the game being played. So the lads, being what they are, went out on the town to parties with Yorkshire supporters and God knows who else. It was a well known fact that many of us went to bed at two and three o'clock in the morning feeling certain that there would be no chance of play on the Saturday.

We arrived at the ground something like 10 o'clock, with eyes like piss holes in the snow, only to be told that the game was on. We were as unprepared as the Bath wicket at that time. The Surrey lads, on the other hand, had been treated like a football side in the Wembley Cup Final. They were taken to a secret hotel for the night, which not even their wives knew about. All this while the Yorkshire lads were playing it up and enjoying themselves! Of course that's the way we played the game in the sixties, we played to enjoy it, we had many laughs, singsongs and drinking parties, some really great times. Surrey, I believe, won the toss and asked Yorkshire to bat. Geoff Boycott probably played the best innings of his life scoring 146, which is still a record score in a final

to this day – a great innings. Many people say it was the innings of the match, but for me the best innings was played by Brian Close when he promoted himself to number three, went in and made 70, taking the Surrey attack apart on a slow softish sort of wicket. I remembered at this time about the champagne stacked in the Surrey dressing room by their cricket supporters, which the lads had told me was to be drunk once they had won the cup. So I popped along there and suggested that it had been delivered to the wrong dressing-room. Some of their cricket supporters were present and laughed their heads off and said, 'Sorry, Fred, it is still full stop for you in the final, Surrey will beat you.' Well, we went on to make a record score of well over 300 and I knew then that Surrey were struggling. I played a fairly major role in getting three wickets in one over, that of Edrich, Smith and Barrington for nought, which really put the skids on them. Ron Tindall was the only Surrey batsman

to score any runs, 57, and Ray Illingworth took five wickets for 29 runs. Of course we had won the Gillette Cup. I laugh now when I think of those same cricket supporters grabbing the champagne out of the Surrey dressing-room, rushing it down the corridor into the Yorkshire dressing-room. I must admit we didn't grumble.

Later that same night after the celebrations at Lord's we were treated to a party on stage by *The Black and White Minstrels*. We were great friends

The John Player League

The John Player League, an idea taken from the International Cavaliers, was introduced in 1969. Once again this is where I fall out with the cricket authorities, who when they talk about their concern for the welfare and well-being of county cricketers are prepared to take actions which are detrimental to that cause. The International Cavaliers was a game devised by older retired players, sponsored and backed by a cigarette company, Rothmans

International. It became known as the Rothmans Cavaliers. The old players who had given their life to the game were still able to pick up valuable income up to £1,000 per year, playing in the Cavalier matches. It became so big and so popular that the hierarchy pinched the idea from these men and got the current players to agree to play in the League so that they wouldn't be able to play in the Cavalier matches. It meant that men who had given their lives to cricket were once again discarded like trash on a trash heap.

at that time with Leslie Crowther, the late Tony Mercer, John Boulter and Dai Francis. What a party we had. I can remember coming up the Brompton Road at four o'clock in the morning singing clean Yorkshire ditties (I don't know any others), hoping to God that the police didn't pick me up. What the hell, we had won the Gillette Cup – though there was a small drama to follow. When I arrived at Scarborough I was carrying the Gillette Cup because Brian Close had stayed in London on some business and told me to take the Cup to the ground on the Wednesday morning. The Chairman of the Yorkshire County Cricket Club said, 'I hear you have the Gillette Cup, bring it down at once.' I said, 'My Captain is the boss of that Cup and he told me to take it to the ground on Wednesday morning and it stays in the safe until Wednesday morning.' He couldn't say a word to me. We had won the Gillette Cup – although he did tarnish it a little. Of course I never got to the final again. I would have loved to dearly because for me the Gillette is the best one-day competition we have and its introduction was a turning point in the history of the great game.

Do you realise – if cricket was ever sponsored by Wilkinsons, the sword people, nobody would ever be run out, they would only be run through!

Editor's Note

Fred once captained the Cavaliers at Derby and his side consisted of a number of overseas players. Some were from the West Indies and some from Pakistan. I asked him for his batting order and he replied 'Black, white, black, black, white – I'll give you the other colour order later'.

A NEGATIVE BOWLER (0-217)

The John Player League provides the right type of cricket to entertain the crowd and *should*, in my opinion, be played by the older and more experienced cricketer. To turn it into a serious competition as it is now, purely for the monetary gains of the county game, I think is wrong. I see so many players these days taking bad habits from the bad shots they play in the Sunday League into the three-day and Test game. When I watch the Sunday League I get a feeling that this crash bang wallop might be all right for the person who, for some unknown reason, has forgotten the skills and finesse of the game. But who wants to watch that type of cricket purely to see a result? If it's what satisfies people so be it. I suppose it brings revenue into the game but I'm afraid of the resultant effect on the watchers. What I do notice when I play against school sides or even league sides, is that the first thing that happens after five or six overs have been bowled is the setting of negative fields. The whole idea of

attacking cricket has vanished and kids, through watching television or watching the one-day game live, are starting to play the game in the same way. After six overs there are no slips. Everybody is into a defensive position and the bowler is trying to bowl short of a length to keep the runs down. If our kids in our schools start with this type of defensive mindedness, God help cricket.

I also see this negative bowling coming into county cricket – no longer the attacking game which is the game I feel is more beneficial both to players and spectators. It's on these lines that I criticise the one hundred over limit in the first innings of a county championship match, because this defensive bowling from the one-day cricket can be taken and put into practice in the county game. They used to say that the only two players belonging to the same side anywhere near the cricket pitch itself are the bowler and the wicket keeper. Now there is only one, the wicket keeper stands so far back on so many occasions to make sure that if anything does go down the leg side he is in a position to get across to stop it, purely to keep the runs down. For me, it has taken the effectiveness out of bowling because today it is just as easy to get a side 160 for none as it is to bowl them out for 161. You have taken no wickets but you have achieved exactly the same purpose by limiting the side to 160 for none. When I played in one-day cricket, people came to me to say, 'Well bowled', and I would say, 'Well, I got nobody out', and they would say, 'Yes, but they only took 17 runs off you and that's just as good'. All these are, to my mind, examples of negative play. When people start talking this way we are starting to get away from the basic ideas of the game which was really formed to be an entertainment through skills from the different players. Many sides are playing all seam bowlers and I stick to what I said before, that this one-day game with its present attitude is the beginning of the end for the genuine slow bowler who is not afraid to give the ball air and induce the batsman to play his shots.

It's a load of cobblers to say that one-day cricket cannot train players to play five-day Test cricket. That's like saying that a footballer shouldn't play extra time. It's exactly the same principle because he has only been primed to play 45 minutes the first half, and 45 minutes the second half – I mean players are players. What you are saying really is that someone like Geoff Boycott, a man who plays three-day and five-day cricket won't be able to play one-day cricket.

When I played at Bradford for Derbyshire in the John Player League against my old county, Yorkshire, I took the field with my mate the editor, Fred Rumsey, and we proceeded in the early part of the match to take four wickets between us. The headline in *The Guardian* the following day read, 'Trueman plays for Derbyshire against Yorkshire at Bradford', and opened with the comment, 'To see Fred Rumsey and Fred Trueman take the field yesterday at Bradford was less like the John Player League, more like *All Our Yesterdays*.'

The John Player League also gives a false impression to people who have to rely on the papers for information. The selectors suddenly see that somebody has taken five wickets and the following week he has got five again They say we must go and watch this man. What they forget is that when he comes to the last seven or eight overs and the opposition have got say five or six wickets in hand — it is all crash-bang-wallop. A man can finish up with five wickets for nothing and someone will say he must be bowling well! They forget to take into consideration that the risk taken by the batsmen hitting across the line of the ball, which is the thing they are

taught not to do in their early coaching days, has given this man wickets. He hasn't taken them, they have been given. The only thing he has done is probably bowled straight, which is not a bad thing, but people hitting, getting caught right out on the boundary against medium-paced bowlers is not cricket for me. As far as I'm concerned the batsmen, in cases like this, have surrendered their wickets to the bowler, he has not taken them through his own skills. The limited run up has not helped the bowler. Some people can bowl off different run ups and some can't. It is very difficult to change one run to another and it is the bowler once again in these one-day matches who is being impeded to the advantage of the batsmen. If a bowler has been bowling in a county match at 6.30 p.m. on Saturday night off his normal long run and then is subjected to a change at two o'clock the following afternoon, you can imagine it isn't easy. I think that the Sunday League ought to play one hour later or start one hour earlier and allow bowlers to run off their proper run ups and bowl at their proper speeds. This might bring more bite into the bowling than it has at the present moment.

The Benson and Hedges Cup

That John Hedges, or is it Ivy Benson, or is it Players and Hedges – anyway they do a marvellous thing for cricket. As far as I am concerned sponsorship is a marvellous thing for cricket. More people go to a one-day game than ever go to a county match. I feel that eventually, although it is wrong to talk about it in this book (but I am going to), that sponsorship will come into football in as equally a heavy way as it has come into cricket. You will get football teams who will be actually sponsored by Vauxhalls or somebody like that. I used to play right mud guard for Vauxhalls in the early days. Sponsorship is the only thing that's left unless millions of pounds are granted by the governments both local and national, and that's not likely to happen. You can have a sports council and a Minister of Sport (who is a very, very nice man, because he is taller than me) but you can't expect them to dip into their money bags. I know that Dennis Howell is known as old virgin pockets, so you won't get any money out of him. It will have to come out of sponsorship or charity, and charity begins at home – that is why my wife is so well dressed.

No one can criticise the Benson and Hedges or the Gillette Cup competitions the way I have criticised the John Player League for the limited run ups, because in the Gillette Cup and Benson and Hedges the bowlers are not impeded. They are allowed to bowl correctly by running off their full run ups. The bowler has just as good a chance of using his skill against the batsmen's skills in these competitions and, as I mentioned earlier does not suffer from the upper hand the batsman receives by these bowling restrictions.

If the major championship was a one-day affair, the grounds would be packed two or three days a week. Play four days if you must to train Test players, but get your income out of the one-day match and charge properly. The only time cricket is played to a crowd now, outside of Test cricket, is during a sponsored game. It's the one-day game that the crowds want to cheer, they can't cheer for three days, they haven't got the wind.

The one thing that I find players complain about is the amount of travelling involved in these matches. Sometimes you find them playing at Old Trafford on Saturday and having to travel to the other side of Essex for Sunday. They don't start

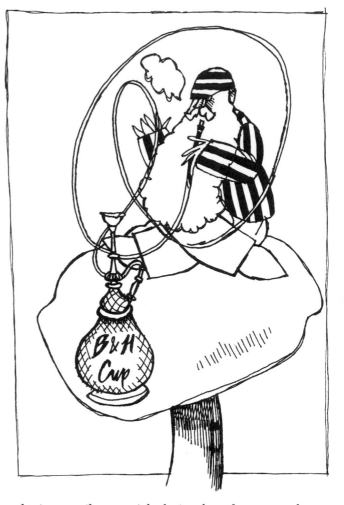

playing until two o'clock in the afternoon, they finish again at 7 p.m., they are away at 7.30 p.m. and then they have to drive all the way back to Old Trafford to continue their county match there on the Monday. Some sort of scheme has got to be worked out whereby the visiting side for the county match at the weekend stays and plays against the same side on the Sunday. For instance, say it was Hampshire playing against Yorkshire at Bradford. Well, it would be quite easy for Hampshire to play Yorkshire on the Sunday at Leeds, which is only eight miles away. It would cut out this terrible travelling problem and not detract much from the entertainment.

It is making the players tired and a bit fed up having to give up their Saturday and Sunday nights, particularly when they are travelling when traffic is at its heaviest. I am dreading the day when there is a bad accident caused by sheer tiredness of cricketers who are driving long distances on Saturday and Sunday evenings after concentrating on batting, bowling and fielding and trying to keep the runs down.

The Single Wicket Game

All kinds of cricket have been played but as far as we know, the first mention of the word cricket was down in Marseilles in France, when it was called *criquet*. None was more popular in the early days than the single wicket game. When I say single wicket, that means one man against another. Sometimes they only had five fielders, but when people like myself played in more recent times we did have a full team fielding. It used to be played over two innings, something like five overs each innings, or even an eight over game. Many famous men played the game well, notably of course the great man himself, Doctor W. G. Grace. In Yorkshire there was a man by the name of George Freeman, nicknamed the 'Borough Bridge Terror', and people came from all over to challenge him. They played for what in those days was big money, something like 100 guineas a match. Sometimes somebody sponsored him for 200 guineas and when open challenges were taken up the betting that took place on the side was absolutely terrific. So there is nothing really new about single wicket cricket, because if we go back into the history of the game a lot was played before the counties were formed into the County Championship that we now know. I must admit I would like to see a well run single wicket championship, open to all cricketers the length and breadth of the land.

Double Wicket Cricket

Double wicket cricket is played all over the world and there is one big championship which takes place in South Africa every year. Top players are invited to attend this tournament, played for a purse of £5,000. You can imagine the needle that takes place when men are playing for that sort of money, which even by today's standards is considerable. I remember touring Australia in a double wicket competition with my partner, Basil D'Oliveira. We played against teams from different countries, people like the Pollock brothers from South Africa,* Rohan Kanhai and Charlie Griffith, Wes Hall and Garfield Sobers from the West Indies, Bill Lawry and Doug Walters from Australia. Betting books were set up all over the country and the favourites to win it were quite rightly Garfield Sobers and Wes Hall. The fact that they were the second-best side in the competition didn't deter them from winning and some people won a lot of money on them. As in single wicket cricket, gambling seems to play a major part in the game.

*I remember seeing written on a wall in South Africa, 'Ackles to the Pollocks.'

Indoor Cricket

There are now experiments taking place on six-a-side indoor cricket. I have seen this game played and know a little bit about it. It is primarily league cricket with one knock-out competition, although this varies from area to area. Rules are similar to normal cricket except for the limit of overs for both batsmen and bowlers. Incidentally, the bowler is not allowed to bowl short or down the leg side. The batsman can score off the walls, and to see 300 runs scored in an hour is a thrilling and exciting experience.

First of all, to play indoor cricket you must have a very large home. You have eight players in your living room, the two umpires in your toilet, and the scorer is upstairs with your wife keeping a record.

I bet you couldn't field as well in your living room, Eric! The fielding is of a very high calibre and unlike the normal game the spectator is right on top of the play and can see it at close hand. It is something I can see coming along now we are looking for employment for our county cricketers to satisfy the off-season period. We could form a county championship league of six-a-side indoor cricket that would take our cricketers right through the winter, and also provide a thrilling spectacle. I feel sure that sponsorship would be available. I hope something like this does come along to keep our future cricketers happy during the winter and in some form of full employment, because I, for one, would enjoy the experience of watching.

I like the idea of indoor cricket – I'm serious – at somewhere like Earls Court or Wembley. Obviously the rules would have to be changed to suit the venue.

University Cricket

The universities have played a very important part in the general promotion of cricket. In fact over the centuries they have been the nursery for some of the finest batsmen we have ever seen. When I first played county cricket way back in the late 1940s, my first, first class match was against Cambridge University and in the side at that time were John Dewes, Herbert Doggart, Peter May, Doug Insole and Trevor Bailey. Some of the greatest names in first class cricket were involved with the universities and not all of them from this country. There were players like Kardar of Pakistan and Martin Donnelly, the great New Zealand left-hander. The universities really were hot beds for future international cricketers. Now these days, sorrowfully, there are not the same number of good players coming out of the universities into county cricket. Perhaps the emphasis on the academic side prevents the good players from spending a lot of time on the cricket field. Whatever the reason it is sad.

Fenners was possibly one of the best wickets in the world which is very much to a young batsman's advantage. The worst thing that can happen to a young player learning the game is to play on bad wickets where the ball lifts and hits him in the mouth or breaks a jaw or a nose or knocks some teeth out. It tends to frighten him off, take away his confidence. Playing against the universities gave county teams a great opportunity to rest their top players and build and introduce youngsters. Brian Close, Frank Lowson and myself all played our first match on the same day against Cambridge University way back in 1949.

When I was in the RAF I played with that wonderful man Alan Shirreff. He was our captain. He always had a little something against Yorkshiremen but I could never find out what it was till one night after a few drinks he told me. When he was a young man at Cambridge University before the war he was in the Cambridge side, they were playing against Yorkshire and Shirreff was batting. Behind the wickets was a character by the name of Arthur Wood, who was a wonderful joker. At first slip was one of the best slip fielders I have ever seen, Arthur Mitchell. As Alan Shirreff took his guard he said, 'Good afternoon'. They said, 'Good afternoon'. The first ball he received was from the great left-arm slow bowler Hedley Verity. He pushed the ball back with a straight defensive bat and Arthur Wood was heard to say: 'Very good shot, young man, that looked very good indeed, what a lovely defensive shot.' The next ball he did the same and again, 'That was a very good shot indeed young man.' Now that one was with an even straighter bat and he turned to Arthur Mitchell, and said, 'Ticker', which was his nickname, 'what

did you think of that?' 'Yes', said Arthur, 'yes, it looked very good indeed, nice straight bat, the hand not too far round the top, very nice indeed'. So Alan Shirreff thought, 'These Yorkshiremen aren't so bad.' A couple of balls later, a little bolder, Alan went down the track to play a ball pitched a little wider. Of course Hedley Verity had seen him coming, turned it a little more, he missed it and Arthur Wood had the bails off in a flash and said, 'Now bugger off back there where you belong and tell your mates to get in here quick, we've got a train to catch.' So Alan Shirreff's attitude to Yorkshire is now understandable.

The late R. W. V. Robins told me a story about playing Yorkshire when he was at Cambridge University. Wilfred Rhodes was bowling and as Walter approached the wicket in the second innings, Wilfred said to him, 'You got a nought in the first innings didn't you young man?' Walter said, 'Yes, Mr Rhodes, I did'. 'Ah', he said, 'don't worry, we'll get you off the mark first ball. I'll toss one up outside the off-stump. Just push it for one.' R. W. V. thought that was nice and so true enough Wilfred Rhodes pushed the covers back a little bit and bowled the first ball a little higher and a little wider than usual. Robins, being the man he was, pushed at it for a simple one to get off the mark, just angling the bat a little. The ball turned quickly, he got a straight edge to where slip was and was caught for nought. As he walked past Wilfred Rhodes on his way back to the pavilion Wilfred said, 'That will teach you to take notice of old professionals. Remember that when you come up against me in the future.'

Fred would have liked to have gone to university. I have known him all his life. I knew Freddie before he could talk, not before he could swear, but before he could talk.

The Gentlemen and Players Match

One thing that did happen in my time that I was very pleased about — although don't get me wrong, I'm not a revolutionary or anything like that — was the abolishing of the Gents and Players match. I know that it served a purpose. It was said that it was a Test trial to pick the side that was going abroad to play. The best amateur batsmen against the best professional bowlers. When the abolition took place in something like 1963 or 1964, I was delighted. I thought it was a match that really did not serve any purpose except to say that there are still amateurs and professionals in the game. As far as I was concerned titles should have been thrown away years ago and everybody should have been called cricketers from the beginning. Some of the amateurs I met were far from being gentlemen I can tell you that. I did have the dubious honour of being a senior professional and I captained the Players against the Gentlemen the last time the match was played. The worst thing about playing in the Gents and Players match was the net fee I used to receive — £20. I discovered that other

players were getting about £50. After further enquiries, Billy Griffiths said that they had paid the full £50 to Yorkshire. The club then told me that they had to pay another player £30 while I was away, so they thought they would take it out of my fee! I soon put that right but I never got reimbursed for previous matches. Many times of course a second team player came into the side to take my place who was uncapped and he was getting more playing for Yorkshire than I was getting playing for the Gents and Players. And then I am asked if I would join Packer!

I was amazed that some amateurs allowed themselves to be called cricketers. I heard one saying one day, 'Now that we are all cricketers I suppose it makes us eligible for benefits. That would be helpful because I can't afford to play as an amateur any more but it would look bad if I was to turn professional, particularly after a Cambridge University education.' It was things like this that upset me and made me the straight-talking young man that I became. To me this was some young buck looking down on professional cricketers as though we were of a lower standing. One thing is certain — he didn't duck quick enough the next time I bowled against him.

Peter Parfitt Remembers:

I suppose the most famous of my stories as far as Fred is concerned was related to David Sheppard, when David was just the Reverend David and we were all playing in the Gents and Players match at Lord's. Ted Dexter was Captain of the Gents and Fred was honoured with the captaincy of the Players, and on the Saturday afternoon Ted Dexter, in his desperation, decided that he ought to have a bowl himself at John Edrich and myself. He bowled me a long hop down the leg side which I hooked in the middle of the bat and David Sheppard caught it about three yards from the bat, two inches off the ground. I said, 'bloody hell' and he said, 'I do beg your pardon'. With that I cleared off back to the pavilion, walked up the steps — all those steps at Lord's pavilion into the dressing-room where my Captain, Frederick Seward Trueman was awaiting, and I said, 'I'm sorry Fred but that was a bloody good catch', to which he replied, 'Never mind me ol' duck, let's face it, when that bastard puts his hands together he's in with a better bloody chance than you are'.

The County Scene

BRIEF REMINISCENCES OF A LIFETIME SPENT IN COUNTY CRICKET

Derbyshire

It is said, and I don't know how true it is, that Derbyshire is probably the most sparsely populated of all the counties playing first class cricket. Yet over the years they have produced some very fine players both for the county and for England. It is a well known fact that Derbyshire has had some of the best and fastest bowlers ever seen in the game. That immediately makes me think of one man – the greatest English county bowler in my time – a man by the name of Les Jackson who, without doubt or fear of argument, was the best six-day-a-week, day in day out bowler I ever played against. The most underrated fast bowler of any era. How this great man did not have 50 caps for England no one will ever know. I think he played twice, once in 1949 against New Zealand and once in 1961 against Australia, 12 years later. England had run into injury trouble and the only fast bowler on his feet was me, so they brought back the old war horse Les Jackson. I have often thought to myself how could people like Shackleton from Hampshire, who was a very fine bowler, of slow medium pace, Cartwright, Ridgeway and John Warr of Middlesex, play for England when this man was left at home? I put Les Jackson, as many others did, on a very high pedestal. I feel sure had he bowled with Alec Bedser and Trevor Bailey in Australia in the fifties he would have come back as England's leading wicket taker. The wickets in Australia, hard and fast, were right up his street. He was the only real genuine wicket to wicket bowler that I played against – except possibly Jack Flavell, and when I say wicket to wicket, he got his left foot so far across that his right arm came over the top of the wicket at his end and he bowled

straight at the wicket at the other end. He had the ability to move the ball both ways off the deck and bowl a lethal bouncer. Every batsman at that time feared Les. 'We are playing against Derbyshire tomorrow, we have got to face that bloody Jackson.' This is how they talked when they were actually playing against me who was supposedly England's quickest bowler. What a great bowler he was. Nobody wanted to face him. When you see his record of wickets, playing with a county like Derbyshire where they were many times beaten by an innings, you wonder how he did it. He is, in my opinion, up there with the best of all time.

Derbyshire were playing against Sussex at Brighton and on Saturday night the captain of Sussex, Hugh Bartlett, went to have a drink as usual with the opposing captain from Derbyshire, Guy Willatt. He told Guy that they were having a sort of charity match on the morrow at the beautiful home of a patron of the Sussex Cricket Club, a Brigadier who puts the match on every year and likes to play against county players. He asked if there was any possible chance of say, four or five of the Derbyshire players playing. 'I'm sure that can be arranged', said Guy. 'One thing', said Hugh, 'one man we don't want to play because he is such a good bowler, is Les Jackson.' Les can only bowl one way and that is straight and moving the ball both ways off the seam. He would get everybody out and there would be no game. But he was invited to go for lunch and dinner! Les and his partner Cliff Gladwin enjoyed every part of the day although a little concerned about the pomp of the occasion. When it was time for dinner and the beautiful double oak doors were open before them and they could see the loveliest of feasts that anyone had ever seen – fresh Scotch salmon, fresh Aberdeen Angus beef, asparagus with all the sauces – they were even more concerned. It really was a super spread. Everyone sat down and for starters they had a cold consommé. As they got down to it, Les Jackson took a spoonful of his and shouted right up the table to his mate Cliff Gladwin at the other end, 'Eh! Cliff, we really are alright here mate, they have forgotten to warm the bloody soup up.'

The Old County Ground, Dove Dale

Essex

Essex is a county which, through the ages, has been called the Cinderella county. In the early 1930s, the great Yorkshire machine was rocked to its solid foundations at Huddersfield, when Essex bowled them out – bowled the great Yorkshire side out including people like Herbert Sutcliffe, Maurice Leyland, Wilf Barber – those big names – for a mere 31 or 32. A great character called Stan Nichols was doing most of the damage, taking wickets and also scoring a century. It came to light that a Yorkshire committee man walked onto the ground 45 minutes late, looked at the scoreboard, saw what it said – 29 for 9. He said to a spectator, '29 for 9, who's bowling 'em out, Bowes?' 'No, he's batting', was the unbelievable reply. Over the years Essex have produced some great cricketers. Trevor Bailey must be England's best all-rounder since the war and possibly one of the best all-rounders of all time. Of course there was also Kenneth Farnes, that fearsome fast bowler. I remember Dickie Dodds, a batsman who was not afraid of hitting the first ball over the side-screen for six – a cavalier sort of cricketer who believed in entertaining the crowds. Dickie used to open with Gordon Barker and one year he turned very religious and constantly talked about the light that he had seen. They were playing Northampton at Southend and had about 20 minutes to bat at the end of the day and Dickie was carving at everything, carve, carve, carve, and in about 15 minutes he had about 45 on the board. Gordon Barker, who had faced an over and a half from Frank Tyson and hadn't laid a bat on the ball, called to him, 'Eh! Dickie, that bloody light you've seen, you might shine a bit down this end.'

Doug Insole played for Essex, a type of on-side player. He also skippered them as did more recently Keith Fletcher. The Essex wicket seamed a lot, making run scoring difficult. Perhaps that's why Doug Insole played on the on-side.

It is a well known fact that it was in Essex at Leyton where the late Herbert Sutcliffe and Percy Holmes took the then world record score to 555.

When the score had reached that magical number Herbert Sutcliffe turned to the umpire and asked if the scoreboard was correct and the umpire confirmed that it was. It so happened that Herbert hit his wicket next ball and walked off. It was only then that the scorers found, so the story goes, that they were one run short. A thorough check right back through the record somehow brought to light a no ball or a wide. The most popular brand of cigarettes following this match in Yorkshire, was State Express. All you did was to ask for a packet of Holmes and Sutcliffe and the shopkeeper knew exactly what you wanted.

Another time in Essex a supporter sorted out Trevor Bailey and said, 'Mr Bailey, I am one of your greatest fans. It really is nice to see you in the Essex team. I particularly enjoy your performances.' Trevor said, 'That is very kind of you. The seaming conditions have helped my bowling just lately.' 'But it's your batting that I enjoy most', said the man. 'Is that so?' purred Trevor. 'Yes, I'm the caterer on the ground and when you are batting my tent is full to capacity' was the reply!

What can I say about Trevor Bailey that hasn't already been said? Very little – and that's never been said.

In 1948 Essex were the only side to bowl out the all-powerful Australians in the same day. Of course, they did get 721 but even that score is in doubt because the Australian scorer, Billy Ferguson, went off to visit some friends. This left the old Essex scorer to record on his own. He had a heart attack and so an old scorecard and paper seller, who said he had done a bit of scoring, was asked to take over. At the end of the day it was not certain whether Australia were 680 all out, or 760 all out, and it is said that a compromise of the now famous score of 721 was made.

Glamorgan

Glamorgan – the Welsh county which plays in the County Championship. I have enjoyed many hours in Wales. I have played at Neath, Swansea and Cardiff. I find the Welsh people friendly, with a passionate love for the game of cricket. Almost as great as their love for Rugby – and they are more behind their team than a lot of English supporters. At the present with players like Hopkins, Wilkins, Llewellyn and Richards currently in their side, they have the makings of a pretty useful team. I would not be one bit surprised to see them win one of our major competitions. I used to love to play against Wilf Wooller, no matter what anybody says. Believe me he was a force to be reckoned with. We thought in Yorkshire that Wilf was born in the wrong county. He should have played for us. He played the cricket the same way and that is to win. In 1948 Wilf Wooller, a strong disciplinarian, got a team together that must have been one of the finest close to the wicket, fielding sides ever produced. They won the Championship that year. I particularly remember Gilbert Parkhurst who was a very stylish opening batsman and Alan Watkins the all-rounder, a lovely man. I used to hate to bowl at Swansea when the tide went out, because it would take all the sand with it and the ball would bounce about a foot lower. All Glamorgan skippers know the times of the tides.

Wales is very much like Yorkshire with its mines, hills and valleys – the Welsh just sing more that's all. When Bevan threatened to send prostitution underground it was only to pamper the Welsh miners – although some of it rubbed off on the Yorkshire pits. Glamorgan were playing against Yorkshire at Ebbw Vale down in the valleys one day, near a mine, and Peter Walker was batting. The wicket had had a little bit of rain the night before and the odd piece was coming out. Peter kept throwing bits away when suddenly a large sod came away and left a gaping hole. Peter replaced the turf and knocked it in rather firmly with the toe of his bat. He still swears blind to this day that somebody tapped back.

Gloucestershire

Gloucestershire, a West Country county side. How the club rings with history, starting of course with the father figure, W. G. Grace. Perhaps the greatest story about Grace was when touring Australia, he was asked to play in a benefit match one Sunday and 20,000 people turned out to watch him play. The first ball he received rapped him low down on the pads and the bowler appealed. The young umpire gave him out. Grace didn't move and the bowler appealed again. Again the young umpire gave him out. This time Grace walked down the wicket towards the umpire and said, 'Young man, there are 20,000 people on this ground. They have come to see me bat, not you umpire, kindly get on with the game.' Charlie Parker also played for Gloucestershire. All sorts of players gained England caps. In my time there was George Emmett, Jack Crapp, not forgetting of course the great Wally Hammond. Players like David Allen, John Mortimer, Tom Graveney who went to Worcestershire, and Arthur Milton – all these carried on the Gloucester tradition of providing players for England. And of course the greatest hitter of all time, G. L. Jessop, came from Gloucestershire.

They have been doing very well in the past few years. They have lifted the Gillette Cup, and only in 1977 they won the Benson and Hedges Cup. The skipper, Mike Procter, is truly a great all-rounder. What a pity, harping back, that politics have prevented this man from peddling his great talent around the world. Perhaps Kerry Packer is going to change that. I'm sure many people would enjoy it. In fact it was Mike Procter who took Gloucester to the brink of nearly winning their first Championship in 1977. If weather had not interfered in the other two matches, Kent v Warwickshire at Birmingham and Middlesex v Lancashire at Blackpool, I feel sure that they would have brought off the County Championship. There is nothing like winning championships to foster success and make it pay. People are willing to go and watch sides who

The Immaculate Tom

are winning and the enthusiasm of the Gloucestershire supporters is really something. I have never understood why they have not been able to muster something in the region of 10-12,000 members because the game is very well loved in that corner of England.

Hampshire

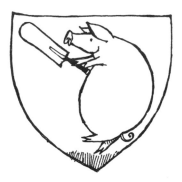

Hampshire, what can I say about them? I nearly always played at Bournemouth where I felt at home, because that's where most Yorkshire people retire to. We had some rare old tussles with Hampshire. One of the most famous, I think, must have been in my benefit year in 1962, when Hampshire with four wickets left and six runs needed to win, were defeated at Bradford. In fact the chairman of Yorkshire, Brian Sellars, went home early, disgusted that we had lost. When Ronnie Burnett rang him to tell him that Yorkshire had won, he told him politely to go away. He said, 'I'm telling you that they have won, we got the last four wickets for one run to beat them.' Yes, of course, I was heavily involved – I took two wickets in two balls and caught the other two. That was all for the good because the next day it was my benefit match against Surrey and the papers said, 'F. S. Trueman stages his one-man show to make sure of a big crowd on the morrow.'

Hampshire through the years have produced some very fine players, Phil Mead is one that comes to mind. A funny thing about some counties – some produce left arm bowlers, some wicket keepers, others fast bowlers and some, like Hampshire, very famous opening bats. In this case I think back of Phil Mead, and then in my time of Roy Marshall, who must have been one of the best players I saw. Roy is now coaching in Taunton, a superb stroke player and very fast scorer who took any attack apart. Most bowlers had two gulleys 30 feet back, and still the ball would flash through them head high. He and Jimmy Gray made a superb partnership for Hampshire – especially in the year they won their first ever championship. It was their prolific run scoring that did the trick, backed up of course by possibly the best medium-pace bowler of all time, one Derek Shackleton. He, once again, had Yorkshire connections, having been born there. What a fine bowler he turned out to be. In fact, I think that he has taken 100 wickets in a season consecutively more times than any other bowler,

YET ANOTHER DANGEROUSLY SHORT-PITCHED DELIVERY!

including the great Wilfred Rhodes. It is only Rhodes, with 23 times, who has beaten Shackleton's 17 times on taking 100 wickets or more in a season. Titch Freeman in fact also did it 17 times.

Hampshire have got possibly the best opening partnership in the world with Barry Richards of South Africa backed up by Gordon Greenidge from the West Indies. It really is amazing to follow their progress, to see the stands they put on and the runs that they score. Mark you, it is not only the scores they make that is impressive, it's the rate at which they get them.

HON L. H. TENNYSON
HAMPSHIRE

One of our ex-umpires, Lofty Herman, who played for Hampshire in the old days, tells a lovely story about their then captain, Lord Tennyson. His Lordship was held in high esteem throughout the county and on one particular day the club were doing badly and at teatime they were about eight wickets down for very few runs. So Lord Tennyson had a team meeting and decided that after tea if one wicket fell then the best thing that they could do would be to appeal against the light and see if they could get the game put off until the following day. So, low and behold, after tea, first or second delivery, someone was bowled and in walked Lofty Herman. As he walked past his Lordship, Lord Tennyson said, 'Herman, do you remember what I said at the interval?' and Lofty turned and said, 'I can hear you my Lord, but I cannot see you.'

We should have flood-lit cricket. I'm sure this would work. A white ball like a hockey ball could be used as long as it's not mine. You could have coloured balls, especially if it hits you hard.

Kent

The County of Kent is the garden city of England. It really is a lovely county. It is split into two by the Medway and there is a man of Kent and a Kentish man, though which side is which I am not quite sure. It is said that they like their cricket even more than they do in Yorkshire. My next door neighbour is a man from Kent – but I don't hold that against him. In the last few years they have been prolific in finding and bringing forward young players. In the future they could well provide for England as many great players as they have in the past – people like Colin Blythe, Titch Freeman, Leslie Ames, Godfrey Evans and Doug Wright. Godfrey Evans said to me that Doug Wright was the best leg spin bowler he ever saw. He said that when he dropped it even on good wickets, it still spun and turned quickly. I had the great pleasure of playing against Doug on more than one occasion. I never played with Leslie Ames, but I would like to have done.

One day a man from Yorkshire was watching a Yorkshire v Kent match in Kent, and Yorkshire were going through a bad time. He was sitting quietly when a man of Kent, or a Kentish man, asked him where he came from. 'As a matter of fact I come from Yorkshire', he said, 'and I am just down to watch the cricket and enjoy myself'. The home supporter said, 'Yes, it's a pity about Yorkshire, they are not doing very well – and such a big county with all those people. Never mind things will soon go right just as things are going right for us here in Kent.' The old Yorkshire bloke said nothing. 'You see here in Kent, we are different', persisted the man, 'not as big as the County of Yorkshire – smaller population and we have a man of Kent and a Kentish man within our boundaries.' The old Yorkshireman, wanting to enjoy his cricket, turned round and said. 'Yes I do know that you have a Kentish man and a man of Kent within your boundaries and as I see it the boundary for a man of Kent goes to Barbados and the boundary for the Kentish man goes as far as Hyderabad. Your bleeding county is bigger than ours.'

CANTERBURY CRICKET GROUND.   Photo by H.B.Collis, Canterbury

Possibly the greatest post-war batsman that Kent has produced is Colin Cowdrey, one of the more stylish and fluent stroke players, who made the game look easier than any other player I have seen in my entire career. The majority will say that the most elegant batsman ever to come out of Kent was the great legendary figure, left-hander, Frank Woolley. Not many people realise that this great man took over 2000 wickets in his career with his slow left-arm bowling as well. Another prolific wicket taker before the war was a man by the name

GODFREY'S IN HIS EVANS AND ALL'S RIGHT WITH THE WORLD!

of Titch Freeman. I have met little Titch on many occasions. I would love to have seen him bowl, to get 602 wickets in two seasons – 304 in 1928 and 298 in 1933 is unbelievable. He also got 276 in 1931 and 275 in 1930. He must have been able to bowl. Not many people knew that Kent missed one of the greatest players of all time. It is said that he was considered not good enough, so he went to play for Gloucestershire. His name was W. R. Hammond.

I think, without doubt the greatest character to come out of Kent was the irrepressible Godfrey Evans. The greatest wicket keeper I saw in action behind the stumps. Where he got his energy from I will never know and the way he kept the side going was marvellous, both in county cricket and Test cricket.

98

Lancashire

Lancashire are, of course, the other county who have the emblem of the rose. In their case it is a red one. To play against Lancashire is one of the greatest things that can ever happen to a Yorkshireman. In the old days they do say that the players only spoke three times on the field in a day, 'Good morning', 'Good night', and 'How's that!'.

A lot of people think that Fred Trueman was born. Fred was never born, Walt Disney drew him.

It is an established fact that Lancashire and Yorkshire have produced some great pairings between the counties, like Washbrook and Hutton. But in my time the most satisfying of partnerships – and I hope you will excuse me for saying so – was the one between Statham and Trueman. To bowl with Brian was absolutely great. What a wonderful guy he is. He was another who didn't like losing and many is the time he must have regretted not being able to help win the County Championship for Lancashire. He would have been playing in 1950 when they tied with Surrey, but it was a great shame that such a bowler as Brian, possibly Lancashire's finest ever, never had the distinction and honour of being in a County Championship winning side. It must have been one of the few things he missed in a star-studded and illustrious career. Brian, who after bringing one back off the seam, which he used to do often and in fact he called it his googly, on one occasion hit someone in the lower part of the abdomen. As the man was whipping his box off, Brian said, 'If I was you, I wouldn't rub, I'd count.' It is not known to a lot of people that Brian did like the occasional drink. Why shouldn't he, when he had been bowling all

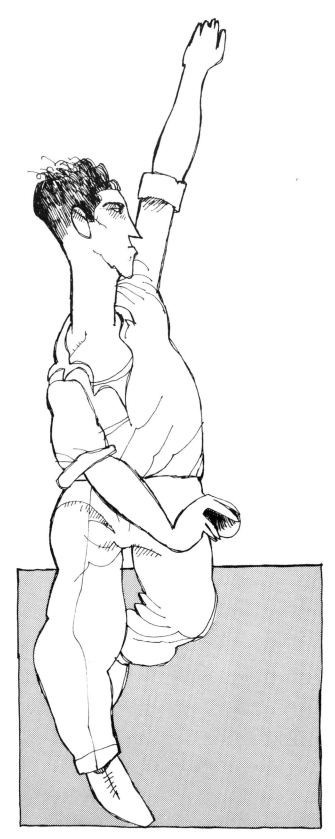

C. WASHBROOK

day. Well, I feel now that the old boy in his retirement from cricket, still as thin as ever, a little bit greyer, is a very happy man. He travels for a well known brewery firm and, knowing Brian's loyalty, and determination, he will be there until he is 65.

Brian Statham was very thin, he was known in the game as the greyhound, he was so slim. In fact it is said that he is the only man in history to get his money back from Charles Atlas.

Emmett Robinson once arrived at Old Trafford very early before any of the other players, looked into the Lancashire dressing-room – nobody in. He looked into the Yorkshire dressing-room – nobody in. He grabbed a cushion, went into the shower, shut the door, knelt down and prayed to God: 'Oh God above, I know thou art the greatest judge of any man and thou art also the greatest judge of any sporting event. Today possibly the two greatest counties in this country will play cricket, Yorkshire and Lancashire. They will meet in combat. Now if Lancashire are the better side they will win, if Yorkshire are the better side they will win. If they are equal the match will be a tie or a draw. If it rains the match will be abandoned, but if you will just keep out of it for three days, we will knock bloody hell out of them.' George Macaulay, a great turbulent off-spin bowler from Yorkshire, caught Lancashire on a bad one, he bowled them out twice in a day and then ran all the way to the front of the pavilion and shouted upstairs to the dressing-room, 'You Lancashire bastards, come out here again, and I'll bowl you out for a third time before it's bloody dark.'

The Lancashire members and their supporters are just as passionate in their love for cricket and support of their county as any other. They love their cricket and like to see their side winning. They do right, I completely agree with them. In fact Old Trafford is one of my favourite grounds. I reckon that it is possibly one of the best seeing grounds in the country today. I have always been well received there. I've always been well looked after. My wife, when she has travelled with me, has also been very well looked after by the officials of the club, which is more than I can say for my own club Yorkshire. Lancashire's passion is parochial. I used to play at Old Trafford and would be bowling bouncers at Cyril Washbrook who was a great hooker although he did tend to hit the ball in the sky. Sometimes he got away with it, sometimes it used to get him out, but he used to like to hook and the crowd used to give me some stick. 'You dirty bastard, Trueman, stop bouncing, cut it out', they would cry. On one particular occasion I was playing in a Test match and bouncing them against the Indians, or whoever it was, and there were the same Lancashire supporters shouting, 'Go on Fred lad, that's it, let him have it. Knock their bloody heads off, it's great to see it.'

I hope through my broadcasting and writing activities that I spend many more happy hours at Old Trafford, because if Yorkshire can't win the Championship then all Yorkshire want Lancashire to win it. If Lancashire can't win it, all Lancashire want Yorkshire to be lower than them. In fact all the banter that takes place at cricket grounds or any other sort of sport involving Yorkshire and Lancashire is really all very good fun. It has gone on for over a century and I hope it goes on for more.

Leicestershire

The fox county, Leicestershire – how that county has struggled on for year after year always producing the odd great player. I would imagine that many will remember Les Berry and the wonderful George Geary an all-rounder. Leicestershire have had one or two useful players like Charley Palmer who captained them and managed a tour to the West Indies; the late Maurice Tompkin, and of course Jack Walsh the Australian left-arm Chinaman and googly bowler, who was possibly one of the best of that type that I have ever played against. They really were a fun side to play cricket with. They played hard and at times they produced some shock results. In fact it was Leicestershire who produced the only tied match I ever played in at Huddersfield in the 1950s. They have had a lot of players on the verge of English cricket, like Terry Spencer who was a fine bowler and unfortunately not able to play for England. Until Ray Illingworth arrived from Yorkshire to skipper them, they hadn't really set the cricket world alight. Raymond got a side together that proved to be a force winning the Sunday League Championship, Benson and Hedges Cup, and for the first time in their history the County Championship. I love to see sides like Leicestershire win the County Championship because it stimulates interest in areas not used to success, which can only do good for the game. Mike Turner, their secretary, has enthusiasm to be admired so that Leicester are now a force to be reckoned with.

It was on the Leicester ground, Leicester v Essex, that they couldn't keep the wicket bound together. It was turning square and Essex had bowled Leicestershire out. The groundsman went to the captain of Essex, Trevor Bailey and said, 'Captain what would you like?' meaning, what roller do you want. Trevor Bailey said, 'Two deck chairs, a bucket and spade and a pair of sun glasses for a start'. Since those days Leicestershire have taken the ground over themselves and have, I understand, produced a wicket with as much bounce in it as any wicket in the country today.

One of the finest cricket brains I have ever seen in action, is in the head of Ray Illingworth. Now the reason I am saying this is because he is sitting opposite me and has given me a fiver. I tell a lie, he has not the greatest cricket brain I have ever seen and the reason I am saying this is because he has left the room and taken his fiver back with him. It was on a piece of string. No it wasn't it was on elastic, that's even quicker to the pocket.

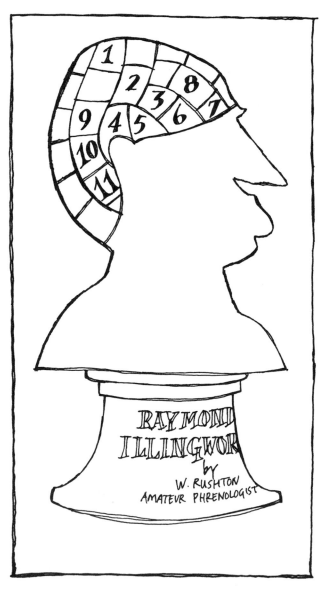

Middlesex

Middlesex play at the headquarters of cricket, Lord's. What a fascinating ground Lord's is. All Yorkshiremen consider it theirs because a Yorkshireman, Johnny Lord, started it all when he built a cricket ground down there for the southerners many years ago. It was built in three different places. The first, from 1787 to 1810 was situated where Dorset Square now is, the second from 1809 to 1813 at North Bank – this had to be abandoned owing to the cutting of the Regent's Canal, and the third, opened in 1814 is where the game is played today. According to *Wisden* the pavilion which was erected in 1890 cost £21,000 then. I always get a thrill playing at Lord's in front of that vast pavilion, whether in a county match against Middlesex or a Test match or currently for the Lord's Taverners in their annual game. To see the Long Room at Lord's is a wonderful sight. It's steeped in history as is seen if you go into the museum or to the library. I think that Lord's has the biggest draw of any ground in the world. Just to walk through the gates, the Grace gates, named after the great man, the father figure of cricket, gives me a thrill. It really has a magic all of its own. What it is I don't know, but it's there.

The MCC have just built a marvellous new indoor school from donations from people all over the world, and I'm glad to see that my old mate Don Wilson, who played for Yorkshire and a couple of times for England, has gone down to supervise the coaching. I can tell them they are very lucky to get this man because I don't think there is anyone better with kids. Thinking back to the ground again with its famous slope – its famous ridge that was supposedly there and had to be ironed out, it was at Lord's where I saw one of the really great Test innings in 1957. I was bowling on this supposedly famous ridge, when I saw Everton Weekes play one of the greatest innings I think I have ever seen in Test cricket. He had reached the nineties and where the ball had flown often and hit him on the gloves, blood was oozing, in fact out of the end of his finger nail. Yet he never flinched and he never complained.

I was watching this and was bowling from the nursery end. I thought if I can bowl one up to him a little bit wide to go away and he's expecting me to drop it short, I might induce him to get a nick to the slips, particularly with a bad hand. So I worked all this out and ran up to bowl. I was wrong. I bowled a half volley a little bit wide alright, but Everton Weekes, instead of playing like an orthodox batsman and hitting it through the covers, put his left foot across and flipped it from just outside the off-stump to just underneath Father Time on the grandstand, for six! It must have been one of the best shots I have ever seen, in certainly the best innings.

I used to like to bowl at Lord's. In fact, one of the very first times that I played at Lord's was for Yorkshire against the Minor Counties in June, 1949, when I took the first eight wickets in an innings. It was then that I decided that this great game of cricket was for me, particularly, if there were places like Lord's to visit.

Middlesex have produced some great players over the years, though they were not always born in Middlesex. An endless list in my time. I remember Jack Robertson, Bill Edrich, Denis Compton then later that great little off-spinner Freddie Titmus, a diehard; another never-say-die cricketer Peter Parfitt – a great mate of mine and John Murray an excellent cricketer. It is said that in the 1930s when Yorkshire won the Championship, Middlesex challenged them to a match because they considered that we had had the better weather throughout the season. Yorkshire took up the challenge and the match was played at The Oval. Yorkshire beat them easily. What the records fail to say is that Yorkshire batted first and due to the conditions, it rained after they had batted, they bowled Middlesex out twice and won the match.

Two of the greatest characters ever to play for Middlesex were the late James M Sims and that wonderful character Patsy Hendren. In fact it is said, that the term Chinaman was created by Patsy Hendren, when he was playing in the West Indies. It was in Trinidad and he was bowled out by Ellis Achong who was Chinese. When Patsy returned to the dressing-room he was grumbling that he had been bowled by a Chinaman.

Jim Sims who played for England and went to Australia in the 1930s became county coach at Middlesex. He always had an answer for everything – was never stuck for a word. One day he was driving his car taking Peter Parfitt to a match when he cut up a trolley bus on a corner on the way to Acton! As he pulled in front the traffic lights changed and he was forced to stop. Eventually the bus pulled up at his side, the driver opened the little side window, stuck his head out and said, 'Eh! mate, you'. Jim said, talking out of the corner of his mouth, 'Yes, what is it?' 'You couldn't drive a bleeding donkey', he said. 'You put a pair of reins on and I'll have a bloody good try', replied Jim. He tells a wonderful story of how as a young professional he used to be sent all over the county for club and ground matches. When he arrived he would announce himself as Jim Sims, the young professional from Middlesex, and poor old Jim might get in at number ten if he was lucky and he never got a bowl. Now Jim being an ambitious sort of fellow got a bit fed up with all this – the old amateurs going in first and bowling all day. So on one occasion when the captain asked him who he was, he said, 'James Morton Sims, Sir'. The captain said, 'Ah! very good, would you like to open?' Jim said, 'Yes please'. He was talking to two youngsters Peter Parfitt and John Murray one day telling them about Ponsford and how he was one of the most prolific run scorers the world has ever seen and that he had, he said, dealt with him successfully on one occasion. He said, 'I was bowling to him at Lord's and I slipped in the old leg break once or twice, then I flipped him a top spinner, then', he said, 'very surprisingly I flipped him a googly and all three went over.' Now the lads had heard this story before, but young Dennis Baldry who eventually went to Hampshire, had not, and completely enthralled, he said, 'You did him with a googly, how many runs did he get?' '229', was the answer.

Peter Parfitt Remembers:

I first encountered Fred when I was about 18 playing in my first year for Middlesex. In those days the senior professionals were always very full of encouragement for you to do well. As I walked towards the crease past Frederick turning at the end of his run, I was waiting for these words of encouragement. He looked at me and said, 'Now then lad, they tell me you can bloody well hook', which didn't exactly fill me full of confidence. He then proceeded to give me the biggest working over I have ever had in my life. He hit me everywhere – he hit me in the stomach, he hit me in the chest, he hit me in the throat. At last I went to hook, got a top edge and the ball hit me straight in the mouth. Off I went back to the dressing-room where I had plaster and everything else thrown on my lip, ice packs, everything. John Warr took one look at it – he was captain – and said, 'Oh, you're all right, you can go in at the fall of the next wicket', which I think was about two deliveries later because G. P. S. Delisle didn't last very long and back down those steps onto the holy turf I went again. Walking out to the middle I had to pass Fred again. He stopped in front of me and said, 'Now, then lad, are you alrit?' I said 'Yes Fred, I'm all right thank you very much'. He said, 'You're bloody lucky, they don't usually come back after I hit them'.

G. O. B. ALLEN MIDDLESEX

P. F. WARNER MIDDLESEX

B. J. T. BOSANQUET MIDDLESEX

M. BREARLEY MIDDLESEX

Northamptonshire

I think most people including the home players wouldn't say that the county ground at Northampton is the prettiest ground in England. Nevertheless it is the home of Northamptonshire county cricket from where some great names of the past have emerged. These were people like Nobby Clark who, Herbert Sutcliffe said, was one of the fastest bowlers he ever played against, and F. R. Brown, at present an administrator of the game, who cap-

tained England on many occasions including a tour to Australia. There were also people like Frank Tyson — definitely without argument the quickest bowler I ever played against — and Dennis Brookes prolific run scorer, Jock Livingston and George Tribe, both Australian. George Tribe was possibly the best slow, left-arm bowler of the googly Chinaman type that I have ever seen and he could bat a bit. In fact he accomplished the double on many occasions.

There was nobody more pleased than me, when in 1976 Northamptonshire lifted the Gillette Cup. I'm sure the club and supporters accept that they are an unfashionable club and therefore it is good for the game, when teams like them win competitions. I only wish that my old mate Colin Milburn had been in that winning side, it would have done him a lot of good. It would have made his heart as big as his chest, he would have been so proud. He comes from Durham does Olly, but he is very proud to be associated with Northampton. Looking back, Northamptonshire was possibly the first county club to be formed in 1820. There are records of an association in Leicestershire by that year and six years later in 1826 an organisation in Warwickshire. It is fair to say that Northamptonshire were reformed in 1879. It is not true to say that Colin joined them from Durham in 1870.

A man who might have been one of the greatest characters in cricket was Colin. He was the right shape, the right build and he possessed some very fine qualities. I feel he would have written his name into the history books of Test cricket somewhere along the line, had it not been for a very bad car accident. Unfortunately, not only for himself but also for England it was a bad blow. Colin Milburn had to have his left eye removed, which eventually put paid to his first class career. But what a character, what a jovial character. He loved a story and loved to tell stories and really enjoyed the game. Once, when he looked as if he was putting weight on, because Colin was up in the 18 stone area, a big man, his skipper Keith Andrew said to him, 'Olly for God's sake, why don't you stop drinking pints of beer and only have halves?' So Olly said, 'Well if that's what you want skipper I'll do it,' so he turned to the barman and said, 'May I have two halves please?'

After the accident Milburn became manager of the then Rothman Cavaliers, and used to look after the players to make sure that they got to the game on time, as well as looking after their needs on the ground. On one occasion we were playing in Lincolnshire against a Lincolnshire side, and I think the ground was Cleethorpes. A very nice man who played for that minor county said, 'Why don't you come back to my house, we'll have a few drinks

BRING BACK DAVID STEELE!

and a meal, you can stay for the night if you wish and go back tomorrow? That's if you've nothing really urgent to do.'

We thought that this was a great idea so off we went. Colin Milburn was driving a great big new Ford Zodiac that looked like a billiard table on four wheels and I was driving my car behind him. We followed the man who said, 'Now whatever you do when you get to my house, watch the drive, it's a very tight turn', and Olly said, 'Don't worry, we shall be alright'. So sure enough it was a very tight turn, the fellow went in, then Olly tried. He finished up getting the car fast on a post, pushing in the back wing. When we got the car off the post and into the drive I said to Olly, 'I thought you said, it would be alright'. 'It would have been', he said, 'if it hadn't been on the blind side'. The man had a lovely indoor swimming pool and Olly just had to have a swim. Some trunks were found that were the right size. They must have been left by Geoff Capes after his last visit, and off Olly went to the pool. He dived straight in, swimming under water for about half a length. He came up exclaiming. We said, 'what's the matter?' 'I've lost my glass eye', was the reply. Well, can you imagine all of us kneeling down by the side of the pool looking into the water to see if anything was looking back at us? As Olly

had forgotten to bring his spare, the pool had to be drained to recover it. Somehow things happen to Colin and with the cost of a new wing, emptying and refilling a large swimming pool, not counting the number of rum and cokes, it was an expensive evening all round. Though the laughter never left his eye.

I think that Colin Milburn is an absolutely marvellous man. He was a marvellous cricketer and a marvellous drinker. I am not saying that just because he happens to be a personal friend of mine. I'm saying it because I am a crawler.

We were playing for the Cornish Crusaders down in Cornwall and Colin was determined that he was going to imitate my run up. He set off from about 40 yards which of course is exaggerated and came running in completely out of breath and collapsed in one of the biggest heaps you have ever seen five yards from the wicket. The crowd laughed their heads off and so did we. It was the world's third great disaster, the others being the Chicago earthquake and my wedding.

Nottinghamshire

Trent Bridge is the home of Nottinghamshire cricket, one of my favourite Test grounds. I thought it was a beautiful ground until a monstrosity of an office block was built on part of it. I suppose the economic pressures of the cricketing world caused it. What a lovely ground though, what legends come from there. George Parr – remember the famous Parr tree that had to be cut down because it got Dutch Elm disease? There were the Gunns and Arthur Carr who captained England against Australia in the 1920s. What about the turbulent years of Larwood and Voce? What an awesome sight it must have been to watch them, let alone face them on those wickets. Trent Bridge is steeped in history. I had the great distinction of taking a hat trick there in 1951 which included a man I'd only read about before the war, Joe Hardstaff. What a character. At Trent Bridge the hospitality flows from Jack Baddiley, the chairman and from Bill Sime the president – what lovely people they are. If I had to pick their greatest character of my time it would be a man by the name of Charles Beaumont Harris, opening batsman. The stories about Charlie are quite fantastic. When people were getting fan mail and Charlie wasn't getting any, it is said that he went home and wrote about twenty letters to himself. I remember once when he was bowling he said to his captain, 'I want a short leg skipper', who replied, 'Where am I going to take him from?' Charlie said, 'I don't know but find one'. His captain said he couldn't have one so Charlie said, 'Can't I', and walked up to where the batsman stood, took his false teeth out, put them on the ground in the short leg position with a match stick under them, and said to them, 'If anything comes your way, make sure you bloody catch it.'

Another time, on a bad wicket, the batsman kept patting the wicket down and throwing the muck off that the bowler had churned up with his follow through. Charlie followed him down the wicket, stopped behind him very quietly and when the batsman turned the other way, Charlie whipped out his wallet and put it on a good length. The wallet had his money in because Charlie always carried his money in his back pocket on the field. He nipped back smartly to short leg where he was fielding. The batsman turned round suddenly, saw the wallet on the wicket and said, 'What the bloody hell's that?' He walked down the wicket and gave it such a whack with the bat that it flew open. Pound notes were blowing all round Trent Bridge. The game had to be stopped whilst the batsman and half the team chased Charlie's money around the ground. Charlie used to look in the paper every morning for his lucky number and if it was 16 he would play the first 15 balls down the line and have a belt at the sixteenth – this was the type of chap he was.

I remember a story about a match he played at The Oval against Surrey. In those days 20,000 people used to watch county cricket. Jim Laker had just got Reg Simpson out and Charlie Harris came in at number three. They had a very dear captain of Surrey in those days called Michael Barton, probably not the best practical captain in the country, but a supreme gentleman. He went up to Jim Laker when Charlie came in and said, 'Well you've got a long on, you don't need anyone back on the boundary for Harris', and Charlie was listening to this as he was making his way down the wicket. He looked at Michael Barton and he said, 'Well, I tell you what skipper, if you bring him in I'll hit Jim out there'. Michael Barton looked aghast, he didn't quite know what to do. He had never really met anything like this at Oxford. Charlie eventually took guard and Michael Barton was still debating what he was going to do, whether he was going to bring his fielder in or leave him out. Jim said, 'I know Charlie of old, leave him out there and we will give him a single if necessary.' 'No, No', said Mr Barton, 'you've got to bring him in'. So in the end he exerted his authority and brought the long on in to mid-wicket. Jim bowled three or four bowls at Charlie who put the block on. Suddenly, he gave Jim a wink and had an almighty swing, got a thick top edge and it went straight up in the air. Who should it be falling to but no lesser person than Michael Barton the captain? As the ball was coming down, Charlie set off for a single. At the same time he shouted, 'Alright skipper, mine', and Michael Barton stood aside and the ball dropped onto the floor.

George Gunn had a wonderful habit of charging all types of bowlers, in particular, fast bowlers. He used to like to march down the wicket to meet the quickest in the business and on one occasion he had a wonderful encounter with Ces Parkin. As Ces ran up to bowl George set off down the track to meet him, Ces stopped at the end of his run, kept the ball in his hand and ran up to the middle of the wicket, met George Gunn and said, 'Is there something you wanted to talk to me about?'

In my opinion the best player of fast bowling I think I ever saw was Reg Simpson who captained Nottinghamshire and of course played for England on quite a few occasions. He always appeared unhurried when playing shots and certainly could not be intimidated. He still has a lot to do with Nottinghamshire cricket and I wish them a great deal of success for the future.

Reg Simpson

Somerset

The County of Somerset is about the most cosmopolitan county in the history of cricket. They have had players from all other counties, they have had players from Australia, West Indies, South Africa – you name any country. Mark you, they have also had some great moments in their time. What about that wonderful Gillette Cup final against Kent? I would dearly love to see them win the County Championship or some other competition. It would be a booster as it has been in Northampton and Leicester. Brian Close, my old sparring partner, has been down there now for five or six years. They are a side that in my time never expected to win anything, but tried like hell to win everything. In the late 1950s and 1960s they brought into county cricket one of the most volatile characters of all time, Bill Alley, now an international umpire. They fetched Bill out of the leagues in Lancashire to play county cricket for them at the age of 40. What a wonderful cricketer he must have been in his twenties, if only we could have seen him then. Of course the great thing about Bill is the fact that no one could ever talk to him, not because he was big headed, but because he never stops talking himself. In fact at one time, Brian Close our captain got the side together and said, 'Now then you lot, remember one thing, if anybody starts talking to Bill Alley when he's batting they will get a right rollocking from me.' We always were trying to send Bill to Coventry but very rarely succeeding. It was generally thought that Bill talked because he was nervous, but I don't think he did, I think he is just one of natures talkers like I am – but what a great character. He doesn't only speak to the players he speaks to umpires as well. Apparently he had a perfect leg-before-wicket decision with one of his little inswingers that he said had pitched right on the line of the off-stump, nipping back a little. The big rough Australian shout from Bill was answered by, 'Not out' from the umpire and he muttered under his breath, 'You're blind, you silly blighter'. 'What do you say?'

said the umpire, and Bill said, 'What you're deaf as well?' I remember Bill coming to see me when I was chosen to go to Australia in 1958 and he said, with a tang of Australian, 'Now then Fred lad, you'll be alright in Australia among the kanga bleeding roos.'

It was at Somerset that I met and really got to know my old mate Fred Rumsey, who is compiling this book for me. It was when he left Worcestershire to play for Somerset that he became an England bowler, something unheard of in Somerset. I can tell you, adopted or not, that county was very proud of him. (He also assures me that had the championship been decided on social points they would have walked it. When it comes to socialising they are way out on their own.)

At Bath near the end of my career the wicket completely disintegrated and the Somerset Cricket Club, who were at the time having slight differences with the Bath authority, agreed that a part-time groundsman be appointed to look after the wicket. The part-time groundsman's main employment was with the AA. On one occasion, Peter Robinson was caught off the glove from a lifting ball and, as he passed the committee enclosure, he was heard to remark, 'The groundsman should bring one of his other signs and put it just in front of the batsman's gate and it should read, "drive with care, loose chippings".'

Surrey

I would like at this stage to talk about my personal friend, the late John Edrich, I know he's not dead, but he's always looked like that. I think that he is a supreme batsman, a very nice man, the same size as Ernie. I know that because of the way he carries his cricket bag.

The County of Surrey – Kennington Oval is the ground and it was there that I took my three-hundredth Test wicket. It is a good ground for Yorkshiremen – Len Hutton made his now famous 364 there in 1938. Perhaps Lord had a hand in that as well. Thinking of The Oval some great names come to mind – Tom Richardson the fast bowler, John Berry Hobbs, the maker of 197 centuries, Tom Hayward, Andy Sandham and the Bedsers. There was also Percy Fender who scored the fastest century in the history of the game in 35 minutes at Northampton. The great names just roll out one after the other. It's nearly impossible for me to remember them all, but of course I do remember the great players of my time – Lock, Laker, Loader, Bedser, P. B. H. May, Ken Barrington, John Edrich, the maker of 100 hundreds. It really is an impressive list. It's a pity that The Oval has the tag of being the unprettiest ground to play on, surrounded by the famous gasometers and flats of red brick. It's not the best seeing ground for a fielder either, yet cricket is played there, right in the heart of London on the 'other' side of the river. It has its own atmosphere built up by the many happenings and I hope that cricket is going to be played there for many, many years to come. It has tremendous traditions to keep up, after all they do hold that wonderful record of winning the County Championship seven years on the trot.

Without doubt the best off-spin bowler they have turned out was Jim Laker, of course a Yorkshireman. The best catcher of the ball I ever saw close to the wicket also played for Surrey, none other than Tony Lock. He caught catches that I believe other people would never have got anywhere near. He was a tiger, a man who didn't know what defeat was – as was the big Alec Bedser, that wonderful medium-fast bowler, who drank, ate and slept the game of cricket.

Sussex

Sussex – the county I always liked to play against. We have had some great tussles with them in our time. They are another side steeped in history. I can think of the wonderful Maurice Tate or C. B. Fry. What about John Langridge now turned umpire? He scored over 30,000 runs and never played for England. Jim Parks and his dad I remember, Jim Parks senior, who once got 3000 runs and took 100 wickets in a season. There was that very fine stroke playing batsman, Ted Dexter, who retired too early in my opinion. I was pleased when Ted decided to come into cricket because he was an entertaining batsman of high class, the type the game needs. Not many people realise that he could have become a first class golfer. Many in the golfing world do say that had he stuck to golf he would almost certainly have been chosen to play in the Walker Cup against America.

John Snow must have been one of England's best ever opening bowlers, full of fire, full of pace, getting into trouble because of his turbulence and carrying on. What people tend to forget is that no fast bowler is worth his salt if he hasn't got some fire in his belly and John Snow certainly has that. Thinking about John, it's ironic that my last Test was John Snow's first. He still talks about it and says that it was one of the greatest moments of his life, that he actually opened the bowling with one of his idols. The editor, Fred Rumsey, says that *he* opened the bowling, not John Snow. (Editor's note – It was also one of *my* greatest moments!)

This leads me to the present-day situation for Tony Greig who has been labelled the villain of cricket by setting up an organisation with Kerry Packer to play what is termed as an illegal Test match. How on earth can cricket be illegal? Tony Greig is a business-thinking man and when he captained England he did a good job. Let's face it, it was Tony Greig who went to India and moulded England into a side to beat them on their home ground. The last time that happened was in 1934 under the captaincy of D. R. Jardine. No, Tony

Greig hasn't done a bad job. At least he is forthright and straightforward. I have certainly got a lot of time for men like that. As for the County of Sussex I would like to see them climb back to their great days, which I feel sure they will soon do. George Cox played for Sussex for something like 25 years and his father before him for something like 30 years, so there was a Cox in the Sussex side for over half a century. George, in due course, produced a son who hated and abhorred the game of cricket, so as a punishment if he had been naughty they used to take him to watch a county match. If he had been very naughty they would take him to watch a Test match and if he had been very, very naughty they used to take him to watch Trevor Bailey. George tells the story of the time his team was travelling from Hove to Northampton and George decided to stay with some relations who lived *en route*. When the team arrived at the hotel the receptionist asked the captain for the number of players who would be staying and he said, 'There will be eleven of us without Cox', and she fainted!

Warwickshire

The County of Warwickshire, they definitely have a ground with the best facilities, second to none. They also have a very good administration staff and through the introduction of football pools they have been able to build a beautiful ground. The secretary of Warwickshire is a former captain of the side who also played for England, Alan Smith, whose first touch of the football in a varsity match at Wembley resulted in a goal. I would say it is probably not a bowler's paradise, but I know one thing, the best Test figures I ever produced in my life were on that very ground against the West Indies in 1963. I got 12 wickets in the match and the groundsman said, 'Thank you Fred for proving to bowlers, not only in my side, but in other county sides, that if a man can bowl he can get wickets here at Edgbaston.' I like going to visit my old mates and yarn about the game, and one man I always look forward to meeting when I go to Warwickshire is that old character, Tiger Smith — what a love for the game he has.

I went to Edgbaston round about August last year with Derek Salburg, who used to run the Alexandra Theatre in Birmingham. It was a Thursday and Warwickshire were playing Hampshire. I went for lunch and stayed for the afternoon's play. There were only 300 people in the ground yet Greenidge and Richards were batting — fantastic players both of them. But they could only attract 300 people for a county match. Had it been a sponsored game the ground would have been packed. Only 300 people! I felt as if I was overlooking the rent. I was in a room with the Warwickshire committee, all four of them. Even that room was empty, the ground was empty but the bars were full. Yet there were people out on the middle running up to bowl their cobblers off, and the batsmen were playing their elegant shots and yet only 300 people were watching and 200 of those got in free.

HOW'S WHAT?

Bob Willis
Warwickshire & England

Worcestershire

Worcestershire is reputed to have the nicest cricket ground in the country. I don't quite go along with that view. For me The Parks in Oxford, the home of Oxford University, is the prettiest. Certainly, if you are looking from Worcestershire's pavilion across the beautiful River Severn to the cathedral, it is a wonderful sight. I used to like to play at Worcester because I found them a friendly bunch who always wanted to get on with the game. Once again we have a county that has produced some fine cricketers over the years. One of the nicest blokes I ever met bowled for Worcester – the late Reg Perks. Rowly Jenkins, the irrepressible, was a well made man and a great guy, always talking. Tom Graveney joined Worcester from Gloucester – they can't come much better. Don Kenyon, though he was possibly one of the best county opening batsmen since the war and one of the most prolific run scorers, somehow or other never carried this into Test cricket, which I thought strange because usually Test wickets are better than county wickets. Jack Flavell, Len Coldwell, Martin Horton – all were men of my time that played for England. Norman Gifford, slow, left-armer is now their captain. He should try to give the ball a little more air. I have had some pleasant days and some pleasant nights in Worcester. You can get into those little pubs and bars that are around the town and talk to people who love to talk about the game of cricket. Of course Basil D'Oliviera too. I remember whilst on the Cornish Crusaders tour of the West Country, Basil was asked if he would like to purchase a ticket for an umpire's ball, and he asked whether it was a lottery or a dance.

Rowly Jenkins was a leg spinner and one day he was playing against a local vicar in a charity match. He played and missed at him three or four times in a row. On the fifth ball he edged one through the slips for four. The exasperated Rowly stood with his hands on his hips in the middle of the pitch and said, 'Vicar with your bloody luck you'll end up Archbishop of Canterbury'.

There was another occasion when Rowly was playing against a clerical gentleman and having beaten him five times outside the off-stump he bowled a googly which shattered the stumps. The vicar, bemused by the in-spin, had fallen onto his knees with his head dejectedly hanging down. Rowly was heard to comment, 'There is no point in praying to him vicar, he can't help you now.'

Yorkshire

It is said that Yorkshire play their county cricket in a different way from any of the other 16 first class counties. I think this stems from childhood in the leagues. Believe me the leagues in Yorkshire are very hard and very tough. When you go out to bat or bowl in a league match you come up against the old pro who has been there a few years and knows that 6 wickets for 30 runs will get him a collection that might make him ten quid, or more in recent times. It didn't matter if you were a 14-year-old because if he was a quick bowler he would knock your bloody head off and think nothing about it. All he was interested in doing was getting you out to get his collection. I think that is where the hardness and the tenacity of most Yorkshire cricketers comes from. The leagues have been our nurseries for 100 years. Nearly all our great cricketers came out of league cricket, such as the Yorkshire League, the Yorkshire Council, the Bradford League and the Huddersfield League.

One cricketer who started in league cricket and had just come into the Yorkshire side, got his cap and, of course, met one or two people. One day in the middle of February he was invited by a patron of the Yorkshire County Cricket Club to have lunch at the Dorchester Hotel in London. He duly arrived and after a few squashes with his host, entered the dining room for lunch. They were chatting away merrily and having a great time when suddenly our friend couldn't believe his eyes. The head waiter was coming pushing a beautiful trolley, displaying different sweets, including a great big bowl full of strawberries. Now this fellow loves strawberries and in a very amicable way he said, 'Excuse me, are they strawberries?' The waiter said, 'Yes sir, they are'. 'Are they fresh?' the question came. 'Yes sir, they are fresh. They are specially brought here for the clientele who use this wonderful hotel, and in fact they are flown in from California every morning by British Airways, just to make sure that they are fresh.' 'By God', he answered, 'I think I will have a right plateful of those, they will never believe me back home. Strawberries in the middle of February, they don't get them up there in the middle of July! How much are they?' The waiter said, 'They are 37s 6d for a half dozen sir.' 'What?' came the amazed reply, '37s 6d for a half a dozen strawberries? You know where you can stick those.' 'Not at the moment sir', replied the waiter, 'I am having a little trouble with a nine guinea pineapple.'

Two Yorkshire cricketers were talking one day and one said, 'What are you going to do about decimalisation?' the other said, 'Nowt, I'm going to Barnsley tomorrow.'

As you know, in Yorkshire they pride themselves on their players being all born within the county boundary. If not you don't stand much chance of playing for that proud county, no matter who you are or what walk of life you come from. Over the

IT MAKES ONE PROUD — (MICHAEL PARKINSON MAINLY)

LORD HAWKE

to hear speeding driving offences and a very severe chairman headed the bench. The first case was read out, 'Richard Hutton', said the registrar, 'Richard Hutton' asked the chairman, 'are you any relation to that wonderful and great stroke player Leonard Hutton, Sir Leonard now?' 'Yes Sir', said Richard, 'as a matter of fact I am his son,' 'Good Lord' said the chairman, 'how is he?' 'He is fine your Honour', said Richard, 'Good', he said, 'case dismissed'. The next case entered the court, another speeding offence. 'What is your name?' said the chairman. 'My name is John Sellers, Sir'. 'John Sellers, are you any relation to the great Yorkshire captain Brian Sellers?' he said. 'The one and very same, Sir, I am his nephew'. 'Good Lord', said the chairman, 'and you have been brought here for speeding. Case dismissed.' Next a little Jewish fellow also up for a speeding offence took his place in court, 'Ah! yes', said the chairman, 'speeding'. The little Jew said, 'Yes, your Honour'. 'What's your name?' asked the chairman, 'Jack Hobbs', said the little man 'Jack Hobbs', shouted back the chairman, 'Jack Hobbs, how do you spell it?' 'Jac Obs', said the Jew.

It took Yorkshire many years to settle down to playing the one-day competition. We had to be honest with ourselves and do a rethink because we just could not play a defensive sort of cricket. We had to be up there with attacking fields, doing a bit of nattering. What's known as gamesmanship, coughing as the bowler bowls and this type of thing. It took us a long time in Yorkshire to get into our minds that these games were defensive and to get our field placings right. We sat and talked about it for hours. We ran into trouble in the semi-final against Warwickshire at Birmingham and only just made a paltry score, something like 175 all out, which to Warwickshire should have been a piece of cake with people like Bob Barber, Mike Smith and Jim Stewart in the side. We employed a defensive field so well and bowled with such a good line and length that it made them fight and forced them into a panic situation. In the finish we beat them by running out five of their batsmen, which is no mean feat. You know, to win the County Championship is the only thing that Yorkshire was really interested in. It has often been said by the chairman of the club that if you come second in the County Championship, the season has been a complete failure. Knowing other counties, to come second would have been a great achievement, but not in Yorkshire. It gives you some idea as to what they feel about their cricket there. We were told that if you can win the Championship you do great things for industry in Yorkshire, for the people are happy, they go to work and talk about it as though it is part of them that has brought the Championship home to Yorkshire. It is their heritage, it is

years the odd player from outside the county has played, but not many. The most famous of these would be the Captain of Yorkshire from 1885 to 1910, the one and only Lord Hawke who was born in the County of Lincolnshire. The man who said, 'God help the day when Yorkshire and England are captained by a professional', which really was taken the wrong way. What he meant was, God help the day when England and Yorkshire are captained by a professional because the amateur could no longer afford to play! A Yorkshire supporter was going on at a match one day about Yorkshire for the Yorkshiremen. 'We're not like 'alf the other sides yer know. Some of 'em nicknamed the Commonwealth clearing centre and others only want a green 'un and they'll have a snooker set,' or, 'Other counties don't give 'em county caps these days, they give 'em turbans with peaks in 'em.' The other watcher couldn't stand it any longer and he turned to the man and said, 'Don't you start talking to me about Yorkshire for the Yorkshiremen and that their players must be born within the boundaries. What about that famous captain of yours called Lord Hawke? He was born in Lincolnshire.' The old Yorkshire lag, as quick as a flash, said, 'Yes that's as may be, but we do know that he was conceived late one night on Doncaster Race Course after the Leger meeting.'

It has been said that Yorkshire cricketers lead a bit of a privileged life in their own county. How true it is, I don't know and I wouldn't say, but they are looked upon in the cricketing world as gods and stars. One day a Magistrates Court was meeting

their right. After all the great county has won the County Championship more times than any other county in the history of the game. It is said that England is strong when Yorkshire is strong. Over the years this seems to have been proved to be right.

I remember Ted Dexter batting in Yorkshire on a particularly wet and sticky wicket and as he walked down to replace a divet that had been taken out, by banging it down with the flat of his bat, a spectator called, 'Watch it Dexter, mind what you are doing. There are men working under thee.'

Two young Yorkshire cricketers met one of their heroes from way back, and as they sat and listened to the rendering of the stories by this great man, he suddenly said, 'You don't get much money these days. I remember the day when you could get a pie, a pint and a packet of fags for 2s 6d.' One of the lads said incredibly, 'Really?' and he said, 'Yes, but there weren't much meat in pies'.

I remember when I first played and saw the great Len Hutton who was possibly the greatest batsman I ever saw in my life. The first time I saw him bat at the wicket was against our great arch enemies Lancashire at Old Trafford when he made 200 in the first innings and 90 not out, in the second innings. I realised then that I was coming into something very, very different. In those days if you weren't in the ground by 10.45 a.m. on the Saturday you didn't bother going because you knew you wouldn't get in.

Len Hutton is known as the shortest knight of the year.

You have to play in a Yorkshire v Lancashire, the Roses Match, to get any idea of the atmosphere. You never get it from the side or from watching it on television. You have to be out there in the middle to see the battle that really takes place. It is one match that neither side wants to lose and they are going to make sure that they do everything they can to ensure that they don't. There are probably 17 or 18 international players to be seen, eight or nine on each side. The cricket is hard and I think that it gives a great grounding to Lancashire and Yorkshire players who later go on to play for England in international cricket. I know that when I played in my first Test match against India at Headingley on my own ground, we had just competed in a Roses Match and the atmosphere in the Test match was nothing like the tension and atmosphere of the Yorkshire v Lancashire match.

The County Cap and the Minor Counties

A county cap, especially in Yorkshire, is the ultimate for many players. It was said before and just after the war that if you had a second team Yorkshire cap it was worth £20 per week in the league. Once you achieve a county cap you should have no difficulty at all in making a living out of the game. As soon as you leave the county side or finish with cricket altogether, you are contacted by secretaries or other officials, who want you to join their league club. Nowadays many county players leave the game in their late thirties to play in minor county cricket and they find it very lucrative. They play minor county cricket during the week and for their league sides at weekends. Most likely they have also found themselves some form of employment. In one way I suppose it could be termed as part-time cricket. But a lot of players I have talked to who have taken this step have said that it's the best thing that could have happened to them. The game doesn't look after players as well as it should when they finish. A player now can get his county cap, have a benefit, get out of the game and make more money than he can if he stays in it. Something has got to be done about this situation, but at the present moment I don't know what. I have suggested a number of ways to give players an incentive not only to come into the game but to stay in it. We are at present losing a lot of experienced county players, who are taking their great knowledge with them and unfortunately not putting it back into the game – and who can blame them.

The best known minor county I know is Yorkshire, purely and simply because Freddie Trueman used to be down the mine. I was down the mine during the war. I was a Bevan boy. I was in Accrington and never saw the pavements dry all the time I was there. I used to have long conversations with Fred whilst he was down the mine and I was down the mine because there is only a thin barrier between Yorkshire and Lancashire. You know that the best thing that ever came out of Yorkshire was the road to Lancashire.

Travelling

Travelling to county matches has become much easier these days than it was in ours, mainly due to the better roads. We used to have to travel by train. We were only allowed to travel by car on the odd occasion when the committee had a meeting to give us permission. Of course the roads were nothing like they are today. The motorways and link-ups make it so much easier for players to get from match to match.

Talking about roads, Brian Close is famous for his driving stories. I don't think I have met anyone in my life who has had more crashes in motor cars. The only time I think he was ever hurt was in 1953 when he knocked a two-and-a-half ton lorry full of firewood off the road and won his case in court. In fact traffic lights have now been erected on the spot to commemorate him. We were in the nets practising at Leeds one day when Brian Close turned up in a brand new Ford Zodiac, which had been loaned to him for the season by the Ford Motor Company. There was a deep scratch from the front of the bonnet right down across the side to the back wing, about six inches wide. As he came onto the field, Ray Illingworth took one look at the car and at him and said, 'I see Fords are getting to know you Brian, they are supplying you with new cars already damaged.'

On one occasion Ray Illingworth had had a long bowl and didn't want to drive to the next match, so he allowed Dick Hutton to drive his new automatic. Dick set off and kept stalling. Eventually he got it going but it laboured for miles. They finally reached their destination after a number of mishaps which included new brake linings, because Dick had forgotten to take the hand brake off!

I remember driving home once with Dougie Padgett from Nottingham and we saw a green Zodiac motor car half way up a tree. As we went past I said to Dougie, 'Look at that car up there'. 'I shouldn't worry about it, it will only be Closey', he said, and we laughed and carried on. The next day we read in the papers that it bloody well was and we hadn't stopped! We dare not tell him – after all he was a boxing champion in the army. Of course it was the usual story with Brian and his driving – never his fault. There is always this tree that jumps out of a wood and savages him in the middle of a lane.

There was a Professor of Anthropology going around a railway carriage one day and he was telling people, as he looked at their hands and faces, where they came from. He looked at one man, a cricketer, deliberately missed him and continued going through the carriage. Eventually he came back, sat down opposite the cricketer and looked intently. The cricketer said, 'I bet you don't know

where I come from?' The Professor said, 'Yes, I do, now that you have spoken, you come from Lancaster', and the man said, 'No, you are wrong, I come from York, but I'm not feeling too well this morning'.

Watch it, Sunshine.

Hotels

For a cricketer one of the bugbears of touring around the country is having to stay in hotels. Cricketers would rather be at home with a very long bat. They get early morning calls in the hotel around 7.45 a.m. By then some of them haven't got in – I have seen cricketers in full evening dress having breakfast.

One time when the Yorkshire side travelled from Dover to Newcastle by train, they arrived at about 4.30 a.m. to find the hotel that they were booked into was boarded up – doors, windows the lot. They contacted the police to ask what had happened and were informed that the hotel had been closed for five months – which just goes to show you some of the administration errors.

Everybody wants to get to the hotel first to try to get the best room available, especially the fast bowlers. They try to get to the back of the hotel away from the busy roads. I remember once at Worcester, not only did we stay at a hotel on the main road, we stayed by the railway station as well. The trains were shunting all night – and we were expected to play cricket the next day! I was lucky; I had a big room at the back of the hotel to myself. So I should, I was skipper. I finished up though, with players knocking on my door, and Bob Platt, Dickie Bird and myself all together trying to get some sleep. In fact the noise was so bad from the lorries going up the main street, it was said the next day in the dressing-room, when bleary-eyed players arrived for the match, that the lorries were so close you could see their tyre marks on the pillows. Some of the hotels we used to stay at were really bad. Paying your own expenses didn't encourage you to look for the expensive type. Some counties used to make all the bookings and pay all the expenses, which of course would be considered in the wages. If Somerset stayed in a hotel below par, the county would actually pay the players what they called hard luck money.

A couple of years ago Surrey were due to play at Scarborough against Yorkshire and they were booked into a hotel called The Balmoral. It's a famous cricket hotel. I had to tell them at a match just before they were due to leave, that nine months before the hotel had been made into a supermarket. I remember one hotel I booked into early – I was still a youngster and I'd got a lovely room. I went off for a meal in the evening to celebrate and when I came back and asked for my key, I was told it wasn't there. I felt sure I had left it at reception. Anyway I went upstairs to the room and sure enough the key was in the door. When I got inside,

I found the old scorer fast asleep in my bed. I shook him and woke him up and said, 'What the hell are you doing in my bed?' He replied, 'This is not your bed, this is mine. Your bed is in there', pointing to a door. I opened the door to find myself in the bathroom where they had put a board over the bath and a mattress with some blankets on top of that. So the fast bowler of the team had to sleep all bloody night on a bath. To make things worse the next morning at eight o'clock the scorer woke me up because he wanted a bloody bath. It was at that time my relationship with the administration changed.

NAME ONE CRICKET BOOK WHERE YOU END UP IN A BATH WITH RAQUEL WELCH

Everyone has a room mate in first class cricket and sometimes they stay together for years. The thing to have of course is a professional room mate, someone like Raquel Welch. Some of our players come in late and they have to contend with night porters. I mean they wouldn't mind Nyree Dawn Porters, but night porters they find difficult.

The Press and Television

Writing about the game as I do now, or broadcasting on radio and television, gives me a different view – I am now an onlooker. I see many things I didn't see when I played. Sometimes it is too easy to be able to criticise because, as a broadcaster, you have an excellent position to look down on to the play and see things that the captain or his players obviously can't. Even so, I do believe that in my new capacity I must look at cricket through the eyes of the spectator, and not the player.

I think that the press should be allowed to watch cricket.

It is impossible on some grounds to write from a player's point of view because the only way to be able to see what is happening in a game is to sit directly behind the bowler's arm. You can then see what the ball is doing and that gives you a better chance of describing that happening to the listener or the reader. What we do find with some press boxes is that we are looking from somewhere over mid on, which is about 50 degrees from wicket to wicket. If we are at Lord's we are practically looking from sideways-on – and at Manchester, too. The two best places for a pressman's viewing position are Birmingham and Nottingham. The Oval press box is in the wrong spot too, as well as being much too low down. It creates a need to consult. Because of bad positioning you have little chance of seeing what the ball has done, which makes writing about it very difficult. A lot of the time you are having to guess by the position of the batsman's feet, once he has completed his stroke.

Television does a marvellous job for cricket. Unfortunately, on television you can see the game better than you can see it being on the ground. But you can't get the atmosphere out of the cameras when they are stuck in one certain position. I don't know whether any of you readers do as I do when listening and watching Test cricket on television. I turn the sound down and listen to the commentary on the radio from Fred, John Arlott and Brian Johnson – but most of all I listen to Fred. Have I said that right, Fred? Is that what you asked me to say? Of course there is the other way of doing it – turn the sound down on the radio and listen to the television commentary, or turn the lot off and buy an evening paper!

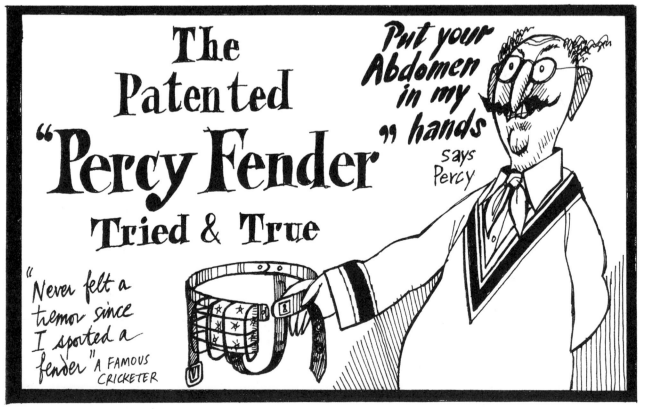

Test Cricket and Touring

A GLIMPSE OF THE FANTASY WORLD OF THOUSANDS EXPERIENCED BY THE PRIVILEGED FEW

People ask me that if I had my time over again, would I play cricket. Of course I would play cricket, I wish I could turn the clocks back 25 years and start all over again. I wouldn't have missed it for anything in the world. I thank God for giving me the ability.

Cricket took me around the world on five or six different occasions and has given me some sort of education which I had missed as a youngster. I would definitely do the same things again and have the same attitude that I had, which was to play to win. It probably upset a lot of people, the way I played, but I was only interested in winning within the rules. I did bend the rules a little bit perhaps, but I made sure that I never broke them. I always thought my attitude to the game was the correct one, playing to win. What's the use of going out on a pitch for five days, wasting all that energy, all that time and people's money if the attitude is 'well, it doesn't matter if we win or lose'. For me winning was the main thing, bringing home the trophies to my county and to my country. I would certainly look for a bigger financial return if I was playing today, because the sport is more lucrative, but certainly not for doing nothing. I have always believed in getting stuck in, effort is always rewarded in the long term, if that is what you are looking for. In my day, I looked for success knowing full well that monetary reward would be around the corner. It happened to me and I'm very pleased that it did.

I'm constantly asked now if the game has changed. It is now ten years since I retired and certainly the game has changed. The thinking has changed. One day it will change completely. I think we shall definitely see four-day cricket played at weekends with one-day matches played mid-week. One thing is certain, there will always be Test cricket.

The Structure of Test Cricket

I talked earlier about the activities of the TCCB, the Board that runs first class cricket in England. It's most important role is the running and administration of Test matches, not only in England but when we send our teams abroad. This in itself is a very big job. I believe the drawing power of Test cricket is the fact that it is nation against nation, something impossible to replace. It's better than wars. It's why we must play our three-day cricket or even four-day cricket like the Australians, to provide the players – to protect Test cricket. Tests must always be played, they are great spectacles creating enormous interest. There are two countries at present who command great crowds in England, they are the West Indians and the Australians, the Australians, of course, being the most traditional arch enemies of all time. The first Test match played between England and Australia was in 1877 in Melbourne, and the first Test match played against Australia in England was at The Oval in 1880. We have just passed the centenary in Australia and are now coming very fast to the centenary in England. When the Australians beat England at The Oval, the bat, balls, bails and stumps were burnt to create the mythical ashes. The winning country, although laying claim, are not able to possess them and if anybody wishes to see the urn it is always at Lord's, where it will never leave.

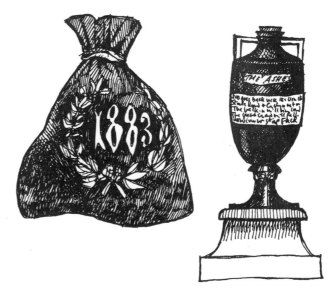

I mentioned earlier about having to keep the three-day game alive or move onto the four-day game. This is so that players can mentally adapt themselves for when they have to play in a five-day Test match, because a five-day Test match needs a different approach. It is more demanding on concentration – especially for the batsmen. They have to get their heads down and play the long inningses that are required. You can safely say that if a side bats for two days in a Test match and scores in the region of 550, the match, usually, will be a draw. The team we have at the present moment is not good enough to bowl the other side out twice in three days. Now that might sound a little exaggerated but it's true. Critics go on about the slow over rate and they are right because bowlers do tend to slow the over rate down in Test cricket, because the game lasts longer and is more demanding unless weather interferes. In England once the covers are taken off and the day's play starts the wickets are left open to the elements. Abroad they are not – the wickets are covered completely whenever it rains, and it makes for a better game.

Like county cricket I believe that Test cricket is sold too cheaply – £2 per day is ridiculously low. I think we ought to be looking for £4 or £5 per day. Let's face it, people go to the cinema these days and will pay £3 or £4 for a two-hour show. When you watch Test cricket you are getting a six-hour show if it doesn't rain, and the stars are live. An increase on their charges could be the first move.

I don't think that there should be five five-day Test matches. I think there should only be one, but it should begin the first day of May and finish the last day of September – one match. It would give Keith Miller and Ted Dexter a chance to win some money on the races, Jim Laker an opportunity to practice for his future TV commentating, Richie Benaud time to go to Somerset House for a name change and Somerset House to go to Richie Benaud for a name change; Denis Compton time to get 2000 runs playing cricket for Greece, Geoff Boycott time to chat up Lilian Thompson, Fred Trueman a chance to take Yorkshire lessons, Tony Greig to get a cramming course or a packer, Alan Knott to get loosened up, Derek Underwood to straighten up, Jack and Trevor Bailey to build their bridge; the Reverend David Sheppard to hit his bishop (as often as possible), Lindwall to write the song 'Won't you go home Trevor Bailey'; Greg to know whether he is Church or Chappell and for Kanhai to wish he could. This game is open to all first class cricketers and Test cricketers in the world. They just play right through and whoever wins in the end gets the ashes for their asparagus. When I die I am going to be cremated and my ashes are going to be thrown at the Chancellor of the Exchequer with the express wish that someone will say, 'Well there you are, now you've got the lot'.

Test cricket is something different, it is the very pinnacle of a sportsman's career, to be able to play for his country. Every county cricketer worth his salt is trying hard to get noticed by the selectors and get into a Test match. To play for England once is something that a player can talk about for the rest of his life. Let's face it, there are many players who have the tag of England and Yorkshire, England and Northampton or England and Gloucester, who have only ever played in one Test match in their life. I think it is the highest honour that can be bestowed on any cricketer.

If you are a Test selector it is always better to be a twin, like the Bedser twins. You see if England is winning Alec goes into the winning dressing-room and Eric goes into the losing dressing-room, but if England is losing Alec goes into the winning dressing-room and Eric goes into the losing dressing-room and nobody knows the difference except by the way they ask, 'What happened?'.

The England selectors always puzzle me. We have a great amount of talent in this country and why they haven't picked Des O'Connor — you remember Des the singing nose? — why they haven't picked him as the opening bat I don't know. Not as the player but as the bat. He's wood right through you know. He's broken more records than W. G. Grace. No, I've broken more records of his than W. G. Grace.

One-day games have now crept into Test cricket and these take place either before or after a Test series. The one-day Test match, unlike the one-day county competition, does not affect the playing ability of the top class players, because they have the advantage of being able to adapt to any sort of situation, having learned the pitfalls on the way up, or they should have. This is another good form of revenue and going back to my last comment about charges, the entrance fee for one-day Test matches is £3.50, nearly 100 per cent more expensive than a day in a five-day Test match.

One of the best competitions that we have had for a long time which proved to be a winner was, of course, the World Cup in 1975. I think I'm right in saying that this idea was born by a man who captained Somerset, Ben Brocklehurst, who is now the Managing Director of *The Cricketer*. For me it was a great competition and marred only by one thing — that was not seeing the South African cricket team in action. I don't think we can call it a full World Cup if a cricketing nation like South Africa is not allowed to play. With East Africa playing in that competition, I'm sorry it proved nothing less than a joke. I could have chosen a side out of the Yorkshire League that would have taken on that team and no doubt beaten it out of sight.

I watched East Africa play England at Birmingham and my words were borne out by the smallness of the crowd then. Here we had a full England side playing against opposition that was rated by spectators to be completely inferior, so they were not willing to pay their money to go along and watch the game. I don't blame 'em. What I think should happen is this. The minor countries should play off in a competition the year or winter before, and the winning side or finalists in that competition should be included in the World Cup Tournament proper. At least that would ensure that the best of the minor countries participated. It could be America, Bermuda, East Africa, Sri Lanka and other countries of similar standing, such as Holland and Denmark. Just think of the boost to the game in those countries if they won through.

The World Cup Final was Australia against the West Indies and a most fantastic sight it was, one of the most, because I wasn't there. I must be honest, I watched it on television at home. I am very fortunate to have a video tape-recorder which can tape things on television when I am not there, like whisky stains. I have Clive Lloyd on my television. He doesn't like it much but I think he is something special – I have never met him but would love to. I remember when Brian Johnson came down my way to do a thing called visit my house, he told me he was colour blind – not Clive, Brian, Brian Johnson. Well, he must be because he went up to Clive once and said, 'Hello Whitey'. I saw Gary Sobers knock his six sixes and gnashed my teeth. But to see Clive Lloyd at The Oval on that particular day, was something that will always live in my memory. On cold wintry days I get a tape out, put it on, sit back, just to relive the moments all over again and bring a bit of summer warmth back into my home.

If Dennis Lillee was bowling at me I would run away as fast as my long legs could possibly take me – towards The Tavern bar at Lord's. Even if I was playing at Edgbaston or even Melbourne. Because you get a good pint at The Tavern. If I was playing in Melbourne and Lillee was bowling, I could be in The Tavern at Lord's in England before the ball actually hit the wicket. The reason being that I am bionic of course. You have only got to ask the wife. I hope you will not want to know what part of me is bionic. It is a little embarrassing because Uri Geller has already ruined my sex life.

In 1954 to 1955 England went to Australia and they took probably one of the quickest bowlers of all time, Frank Tyson. He was certainly the quickest bowler I ever had to face up to and out in Australia, when he was playing at Sydney in a Test match, on a wicket with some grass on it, the ball was really fizzing through. He was bowling at a fellow by the name of Jimmy Burke who wasn't the worst player I ever bowled against. Jimmy was also well known in local circles for his mimicry, piano playing and rendering of songs at parties and at night clubs. This particular day he kept fencing and playing and missing, and after about three overs of this a bloke in the crowd shouted, 'Eh! Tyson, bowl Burkie a piano and see if he can play that.'

I went to a Test match in Sydney once which we lost. It was the year that Ted Dexter was sent over. The Australian feeling at the time was that Ted carried his bat well – he didn't do anything with it – just walking in and out, which was very close between, but he carried it well. He didn't really have time to settle in. We lost the whole series but as far as I was concerned it was a great time and I got to know a lot of England players.

Australia

Playing cricket at any level has always given me great pleasure, but if I was to try to pick the form of cricket that gave me the most delight, I would say it would be playing for England in a Test match, especially if it was against Australia. The first Test I ever played against Australia was indeed a memorable one. That was in 1953 and I played at The Oval in the last match of the series, which we won, bringing the Ashes back to Britain after a period of over 19 years in Australia. Can you imagine the delight? It was always a great pleasure for me to play in a Test match because I felt that I was pitting my wits and ability against people whose ability and wit was just as sharp. In many ways Test cricket is like a chess game.

A few great performances stand out in my time in Test cricket against Australia, Peter Burge scoring 160 at Headingley in 1964, Richie Benaud's six wickets that robbed us of victory at Manchester and the come-back of Cyril Washbrook at Headingley in 1956, when he made 98. The wonderful bowling feat of Jim Laker, 19 wickets in a match, something that I don't think will ever be equalled again in my time, if it is I hope to see it. The wonderful bowling of the legendary Ray Lindwall who was possibly the best fast bowler I ever saw on a cricket ground, a run up with music in it. The three best batsmen in my time playing regularly for the Australians were Neil Harvey, Peter Burge and Norman O'Neil. Bobby Simpson was the best first slip. People have said to me, 'You should have seen Wally Hammond' – if Wally Hammond was any better than Bobby Simpson, then yes, I would like to have seen Wally Hammond. The best bowling performance I saw by an Australian bowler was in the 1970s when the young man by the name of Massie came to England and in his first Test match at Lord's took 16 wickets, which was an incredible performance. The way he swung the ball around was magic as if he had the ball on elastic. But that is cricket, he had this moment of glory at the head-

TWO DEMON BOWLERS

quarters of the game where every bowler wants to get five or six wickets in an innings, and every batsman wants to score a hundred. He got sixteen wickets then unfortunately faded into oblivion, I don't think he has been heard of since.

Bill Lawry, the opening bat who captained Australia, was one of the most difficult batsmen in the world to get out. It was said about Bill, who I thought was a fine player (not only because he is a pigeon fancier) that, like Trevor Bailey and Slasher Mackay, he had no need to worry in life because he would never die of a stroke. When I look at Australia now compared with what they were like in my time it's hard to believe that it's the same country. When I think of people like Benaud and Davidson coming in as low as seven and eight, the mind boggles at what went before them.

Today, although they have one of the finest opening bowling partnerships in the world in Lillee and Thomson, they lack Test match standard batsmen. Lillee, of course, is the classical fast bowler, Thomson being somewhat unorthodox, but, by golly, with lots and lots of pace. Can you imagine a side from Australia with only one world-class batsman? Greg Chappell was the only one on their tour in 1977. It is very hard to believe that good Australian cricket has gone back as far as that. Perhaps a number of good players having recently retired, it could be that the new stars are ready to blossom forth. Good players, though, don't grow on trees, like a lot of people seem to think and committees must remember what I said about one-day cricket competitions. They are not the best breeding grounds. The thing that I remember mostly about Australian cricket is, of course, the Sydney Hill. On one occasion when the Reverend David was batting against Alan Davidson, the ball bounced about three times before it got through to Wally Grout. The Reverend David in a very immaculate way lifted his bat over his shoulder – he did this on three occasions. Then, all of a sudden, a big voice boomed out raucously from the Sydney Hill, 'Come on Alan, lead him into temptation.'

Tony Greig said about Lillee's moustache, 'The last time I saw anything like that on a top lip, the whole herd had to be destroyed.'

Editor's Note
Freddie Trueman was playing in Adelaide in the fourth Test which coincided with the Foundation Day public holiday. Just beyond the confines of The Oval there is a parade ground where they have a 26-gun salute which starts exactly at noon. It coincided with Fred being at the end of his run and when the first boom went off Fred grabbed himself around the heart. A little later a second one went off and Fred staggered, and when the third one went off he collapsed prostrate to the ground! The next thing you see is that out of his pocket comes a little white handkerchief which he gently waves.

Tours are hardships not all cricketers enjoy, particularly tours to countries where the whisky is more palatable than the water. Not everyone has had my basic training, due to coal dust on the lungs at a very early age. The success of any tour both on and off the field depends on whether or not the tour team is good enough. I remember a tour in the good old days of the amateur and professional that left these shores for Australia with a duke, nine men good and true, seven amateurs, including a clerical gentleman, a model agency and six bags of golf clubs. I'm still not sure whether we were under Jockey Club rules, on the golf convention's outing, Dexter's Enterprises or a bloody missionary hunt.

Editor's Note
It has been reported that the Reverend Gentleman was generally met at airports by others of his calling. On one occasion at Sydney the plane was met by a bishop and a nun. Fred, from the rear of the aircraft was heard to call to the Reverend David in the front, 'Eh! up Rev, not only has the senior pro come to meet you, but he's fixed you up as well.'

The West Indies

The West Indies for one minute are on top of the world and the next they have all grown old together and they are down. Suddenly they will bounce back again with a new collection of stars. What about the way the West Indies bounced back in England in 1976 after a strenuous all-the-year-round cricket trip that took them through India, Pakistan, Australia and New Zealand, back to the West Indies then across to England. They came over and played some of the most fantastic cricket I have ever seen. New stars were born then. This fellow Viv Richards must surely now be competing with his namesake Barry for the role of best batsman in the world today. At the age of twenty-four he was already matured, he has timing, he has style, he has class. I don't think we have seen the last of this man, he might well become a legend before he is 30. Now what about their bowling? When you think of Michael Holding, Wayne Daniel and Andrew Roberts all in one side, it's a frightening thought.

Why should they need spin bowlers on good Test wickets when they've got three bowlers with such an awesome pace that these can generate. When Daniel and Holding were unfit they immediately unearthed two more bowlers almost as good. One in particular, Colin Croft, went on to get over twenty wickets in his first series.

I like the West Indies; they make me laugh. I mean how can you play cricket in Barbados? What do they know, you need the sun and warmth to play it properly.

The West Indies are rich in talent because cricket is more than their national game, it is a religion to them. They are brought up to play on good wickets and, as I said before, that's where batsmen gain their confidence. In fact it improves bowlers because they have to try harder. When I first saw the great Gary Sobers in 1953 I wouldn't have put my money on him becoming a batsman of the highest class that he reached. In fact I think it would be fair to say that Garfield Sobers became, by the end of his career, the greatest all-rounder of all time. After the Test match at Lord's in 1963 when Brian Close put his body before the bat and Wesley Hall and Charlie Griffith hit him all over, Brian had a photograph taken of his body showing all the bruises. It appeared in newspapers all over the world. A few days later when playing against Sussex, Wesley Hall received a letter calling him a big black bear. Wesley said to Charlie Griffith, 'I think this letter is for you. They have written it to the wrong man.'

Spring is here once again and soon we will thrill to the sound of leather hitting Brian Close.

I remember playing festival cricket at Scarborough against the West Indies. At the end of play I went into the dressing-room to ask the lads what they were going to do in the evening. Somebody suggested that the theatre was a good idea. They asked me what shows were appearing and I reeled them off including *The Black and White Minstrel Show*. Wes Hall said, 'Man, there's no reason to go and see a show like that, we have just put our own on out there.' West Indians are very jovial people who love their cricket.

I played against a man who went by the name of Cha Cha Forbes, who eventually finished up playing for Nottinghamshire. He was extremely dark in colour and he told me a lovely story about himself one night in Jamaica. After taking his girl friend home he was riding his bike without any lights. Suddenly the local constable shouted, 'Who's that man with no lights on his bike?' Carlton said, I had to think fast, so I opened my eyes wide and flashed my teeth. The copper shouted across, 'That's better man, why didn't you put 'em on before?' The great Wesley Hall, who is as black as any man I have seen, said to Carlton Forbes once, when playing against him at Nottingham, 'Cha Cha, I think you

are the blackest man I have ever seen in my life, in fact I would go so far as to say, you'se colour is as blue as grape.'

When I was young cricket taught me the three W's, Weekes, Worrell and Walcott, who I thought were quite fantastic. But nowadays, in my early dotage, it's not Weekes, Worrell and Walcott, it's women, wedlock and worry.

Pakistan

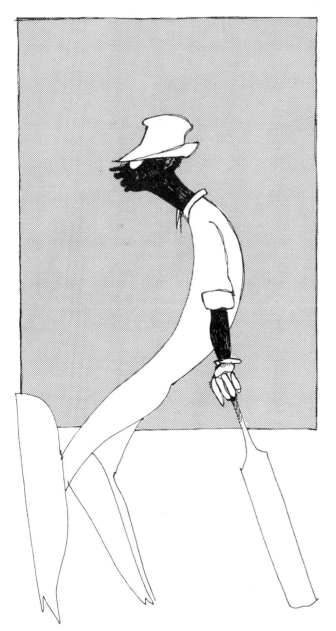

Pakistan is a much improved cricket nation which should now be looking for a five-match tour when visiting England. One of the things I have never understood is the actual planning of the series. We play five matches against Australia and the West Indies and play down the importance of the other countries by only playing them in a three-match series. Pakistan deserves a better fate than this. They have some very fine cricketers in Sadiq, Zaheer, Mushtaq, Asif and Majid – players who would hold their own in any national side. In recent years even their opening bowlers have improved and they are finding new blood as each season comes along. I am sure that the British public would enjoy watching these players take on the might of England over a full tour, politics allowing. These days everyone wants to play cricket in Pakistan. In my day nobody wanted to go, I think the authorities are keen to encourage tours because of the big crowds that they now get there. It shows the growing interest in the game at top level which is something vital to promote. We must consider carefully all the different methods of improving the stability of Test cricket. Perhaps we should play Test cricket on Sunday as they do in Pakistan – and in Australia and India for that matter. We seem to be lagging far behind in this country, although it is the Lord's Day Observance Society that objects to us playing on Sundays in the morning, and have only agreed to the John Player League if it starts after lunch. I wonder if that is a majority thought, not that I am not a God-fearing man. I believe in God and always will, but we have to move along with modern times. Those people who want to go to church on Sunday mornings will still go, and those who want to go to church on Sunday evenings will also still go. Cricket or any other sport played on Sunday will not change the people who worship God.

India

Throughout the history of Test cricket India have produced many fine players, but in my time I'm afraid that I have to be very honest and say that they didn't have a very good side. Possibly the best leg spin bowler I have played against came from India, Gupte, and a lot of players would agree with me. The late Frank Worrell from the West Indies said he was definitely the best he had played against. He just bowled all day, dropped it on a length and hardly bowled a bad delivery, which is what you have to do to be really good bowling leg spin. Manjrekar made a hundred in his first Test match for India against England at Leeds in 1952, but generally funny sides have come from India. Since 1952 nobody really has been completely outstanding although there have been some fine ones.

They have the best spin bowling attack at the moment in Venkat, Bedi and Chandrasekhar, backed up by Prasanna, but they are not a side that I would go rushing to a Test ground to see. I don't mean that in a detrimental or nasty way but the Indians play cricket with a lazy sort of lackadaisical attitude. They are not worried about the crowds, whether they score fast or slow. Some players will bat all day for 70 and will not be moved by the shouting or barracking of the crowd. They certainly bat to the point of frustration by the bowlers. They will play shots if they feel like it and if they don't feel like it they won't play shots. They are not the most attractive side in Test cricket and could do a lot better if the selectors encouraged players to get on with it and not, as it appears, play not to lose. I wonder why they have never produced a really fast bowler. Venkat who came to play for Derbyshire was on one occasion playing at Bradford against Yorkshire. At dinner in the hotel on the first night he asked for a sweet chocolate ice cream. Mike Page, the wag of Derbyshire, asked him if it was his method of keeping his colour up!

An English commentator said to an Indian cricketer, 'What do you think of Bedser?', and he said, 'I don't sleep on bed sir, I sleep on rush mat.'

New Zealand

New Zealand – here I think we have a bunch who at best could be termed as county cricketers in Test cricket even though they beat England once. They give the game everything they have got, but somehow they never seem to be able to lift their standard. They are a small country in terms of population, something approaching three million. Although South Africa are not picking from a population of many more unfortunately – perhaps South Africa's coaching system is better. New Zealand have produced some world class cricketers – in my time people like Bert Sutcliffe, Martin Donnelly, Wally Hadlee, Tom Burtt and John Reid, who must be rated best of all. Probably the best talked about player they ever produced was a fellow called Jack Cowie. I don't think that Dick Motz was a bad bowler either, Bruce Taylor was a useful all-round cricketer and Glen Turner currently opening with Worcestershire must be the best of their latter-day players. I watch this young man and I think he is a much better player than people rate him.

New Zealand is one of my favourite countries and one of my favourite peoples; they have always been very nice to me and welcomed me whenever I played there. You know one thing, they might not be strong enough to beat you, they know that, but by God they try and they are going to give you one hell of a run. Tony McGibbon was a good cricketer, a medium-fast bowler and a very useful batsman. He was touring India on one occasion and, like everybody else, had what is known as Indian tummy. In other words he had the runs. It got to such a point that he was spending more time in the toilet than he was in the bedroom, so he got a pillow, book and blanket, sat on the toilet and stayed there until the whole operation had finished!

Editor's Note
The weather and the wicket conditions matched each other. Needless to say the wicket was extremely slow and Fred was heard to remark, 'It's so slow it's like bowling a doughnut on a dung heap.' He was nonetheless able to bowl one or two of his lethal bouncers and having hit one of the New Zealand players, the player decided to take evasive action towards square leg each time Fred bowled. Having had enough after about two overs Fred remarked, 'If thee backs away any farther lad, you'll be in the bloody bus queue for Birmingham.'

I went to New Zealand and it was closed.

Editor's Note
Playing cricket at Edgbaston against New Zealand in 1965, the weather was so cold that coffee was brought out to warm England whilst they were fielding.

I remember that. One player said, 'I want no disparaging remarks about this coffee because you may be old and weak yourself one day.'

South Africa

What a shame that politics has been allowed to interfere and spoil such a wonderful sport as cricket. The South African game has really suffered. For years cricket has naturally worked towards a closer relationship between peoples and never interfered with politics. I was never chosen to go on a tour by the MCC to South Africa – one of the things I always wanted to do. I remember playing against Eric Rowan, Athol Rowan, Dudley Nourse, Toey Tayfield – wonderful players – and what about some of the bowlers they have had like Neil Adcock, Peter Heine? Believe me, those two were a fearsome pair, second to none in the world at that time. Then there was Russell Endean, and John Waite the wicket keeper who, in my mind, must be second to Godfrey Evans, always in the right position, missing very little behind the stumps and never doing it in a flashy or spectacular way. He could bat a bit as well, make no mistake about that. In the sixties they had the best side, including Peter Pollock and Graeme Pollock, Tiger Lance, Ali Bacher, Dennis Lindsay, Colin Bland and later and into the 1970s, Barry Richards, Mike Procter and Clive Rice.

Barry Richards has never known his surname.

The coaching system in South Africa is the best in the world because English coaches go over there every winter and continue to produce fine players. What a pity though that due to politics we have not been able to see them or to play against them at Test cricket. I feel sure that they would have thrilled millions of people around the world. Only just to have seen the genius of this fellow Graeme Pollock, who if he had been allowed to play Test cricket for his country would certainly have gone down in history as one of the greatest left-hand batsmen ever. I look forward to the day when South Africa and the world come to their senses and South Africa is allowed back into Test cricket.

Touring Abroad

When abroad touring it is very important that the captain and the manager are in agreement and get on with each other because they are the most important of the personalities, the manager in particular. The first thing the manager has got to do, is to gain the confidence of his players and very quickly care about their welfare. I toured on four different occasions, twice to the West Indies and twice to Australia, and I would say without hesitation that a man called R. W. V. Robins, a man a lot of players didn't seem to like, was quite easily the best manager. You could talk to him, you could put your grievances to him and he was a willing listener. In fact he used to come to my bedroom every morning, sit in a chair and talk to me for at least half-an-hour about the conditions, and what we were trying to do and what we weren't trying to do that day. The manager, I feel, has got to strike up a relationship with his most important players because it's the important players that win matches. If you are going to win a series on tour you have got to keep your key men happy, almost to the degree of molly-coddling them. I don't say that there should be favourites, because after all you are there as a

team. It's also very difficult for a manager to strike up a friendship with anyone. He's bound to run into trouble somewhere along the line, in particular from players who are not yet in the side, because he is the man that has got to console them and keep them trying. Everybody in a touring side has a chance of playing for England on that trip and their morale must be maintained. It is a very difficult job. He is the man who has to deal with all the complaints about and from the players. He has to study the panel of umpires that will be offered to him during the state matches or province matches. He has to be able to analyse which are the best for the Test matches. It's a very difficult job. It could be made a lot easier if players only realised what his responsibilities are. He is representing the MCC and England at the highest level as well as being responsible for the team and administration. In fact he has got to be a complete diplomat and at the same time a severe disciplinarian.

The most important job in a cricket team is the manager. He is not a player, obviously. Nonetheless, he has got to have one great gift equally as good as any player. He has got to be able to stay awake whilst the game is in progress. If he can do this, then he is a great manager.

During my time, captains for tours abroad seemed to have been chosen because of their school backgrounds. This I have often said is a very bad thing. I always favour the Australian method of picking the side first and choosing the captain from it. We have had many captains who have had holidays just because of their breeding. I think a captain should never be chosen for any team until he has had a lot of experience under his belt, having played under a very experienced captain, being groomed for the job slowly, learning from the many pitfalls that exist. I always think a captain has to be able to size up the temperament of his players. Some players can be led, some have to be led, others have to be coaxed and some have to be driven to get the best out of them. Until a player or an aspiring captain has learned these main ingredients I don't think he should ever be given such an important job. Many professionals who have learned their trade over the years, and know the game, resent somebody coming along who is wet behind the ears to take charge. Also it's not fair to the untrained person to be put in such a position of responsibility. I would never look at anyone who has not played the game for at least five years at the highest level, when choosing a captain for such an important job as leading an England side abroad.

I don't think there should be anything like a Test captain at all. I think the crowds should decide who should bat, who should bowl and the field placements, and do it by a series of placards. A member of the team would hold up a 'Why?', 'Who?' or 'What Do You Think Of It?' card and the crowd would all shout back, 'Rubbish'. Then by a majority vote they would say, close in, move long stop, bowl a bouncer, put Fred on, take Fred off, and would be represented on the field by Marty Feldman. He would stand at mid-wicket because he is the only man in England who can watch both ends at once without moving his head.

I felt sorry for people like Ted Dexter, who was a fine cricketer. I respect him as a man and a friend but he was brought out of the university cricket and given the captaincy of England without the right training. Leading England in a Test match, believe me, is no fairy tale; everyone wants your guts for garters. Ted Dexter didn't have Lock, Laker, Wardle and Appleyard at his command. He did have, on a few occasions, Trueman and Statham, but even those two don't make a full Test team attack, they have to be backed up somewhere along the line.

If I was captain of England I would cheat, there is no doubt about that whatsoever. I would do what the Australians do, I mean, they call the batsman all the names under the sun when he goes in – they talk him out if they can. I wouldn't have any qualms about that. I would say, 'Get back to Queensland, it's the way you walk.' I would send bumpers down. I would send bouncers at night because although I love the Australians it's a love/hate relationship. I have been there, it's a very nice country to come from very quickly. You know I thought in the early days that Australia was the be all and end all and I'm right.

As do captains, players also need a great deal of experience. It's no use saying, this fellow has had a good season, we are going to take him on tour. I remember once when I had been chosen to go abroad and saw the other names. I said to the selectors, 'Good Lord Almighty. How have you picked some of these fellows, with a pin?' They replied, 'They've had a good season.' I said, 'Yes, but they are not great players are they?', and they had the audacity to say to me, 'No, but they are very nice people!' When you are going out to try to win a Test series, particularly against Australia, you want to take

I HAVEN'T READ THE SCRIPT – BUT WE'RE PLAYING PHILADELPHIA

28   The English Cricketers *en route* for Canada and the United States, 1859
R. Carpenter   W. Caffyn   T. Lockyer   J. Wisden   H. H. Stephenson   G. Parr   J. Grundy   J. Caesar   T. Hayward   J. Jackson
A. Diver   John Lillywhite
From a photograph taken on board the Nova Scotian *at Liverpool*

the best players available. You are not taking people who are nice, who are only going to be able to socialise and act like diplomats. After all the object is to play cricket, not win votes. Selectors should look at players who have been consistent over a few years, not those who have had just one flash in the pan season, who we might never see again. In most cases, the more experienced will get more runs or more wickets the following year.

Of course I don't know whether many people know this but the first English captain to tour Australia, and quite rightly so, was a Yorkshireman. The fact that he never played in a cricket match was not surprising because his name was Cook.

Brian Close was famed for his swimming. When he was with Yorkshire, we called him the human fish, the torpedo. And of course Brian was always looking for feats of daring in his swimming and diving. On one occasion on tour in America, in Hollywood, we stayed at the Hollywood Boulevard. There were one or two nice young ladies sitting around the pool and I was quietly having a drink and a chat with a couple of the lads, talking about the tour and how we were enjoying ourselves. Suddenly Closey arrives clad in swimming trunks ready for his absolutely fantastic demonstrations. The first thing he did was to put a table at the edge of the swimming pool, take a run and dive straight over

the top into the water. The people looked, one or two of the lads, taking the mickey, gave him a round of applause. He came up and said. 'That's great', and of course he did it again, water flying all over the place. He then got a bit bolder, added another table, ran and dived over the top of two tables and eventually as the daring grew, we finished up with chairs round the tables and Closey diving over the tables and the chairs. The edge of the swimming pool was tiled for about four or five yards and as Closey kept diving over the tables into the water, the tiles were getting wetter and wetter and eventually – we knew it had to happen – up came Closey running like a hare, he slipped on the tiles, crashed into the tables and chairs and the bloody lot went into the swimming pool! The people around the pool absolutely collapsed with laughter. It was one of the funniest things I have ever seen. To see Closey trying to retrieve chairs and tables from the deep end of a swimming pool is something I shall remember as long as I live.

On another occasion he decided that he was going to dive off something like the sixth balcony of the hotel – so, off he goes, through the foyer, up into his bedroom on the sixth floor, onto his balcony and whoosh, he's over and down into the pool below. Now there is a chap stood at his mirror in his bedroom on the fourth floor, tying his tie when

OH, TO BE IN ENGLAND –

suddenly he sees a body go by! It was enough to give him a bloody heart attack. He finished up on the phone to the hotel manager, who called the police, the bloody lot. They were all there because Closey was giving the lads one of his diving exhibitions. But that is Brian, what a great guy he is.

Talking of experienced players reminds me of one incident when the England team were abroad practising at the nets, when a great big dray horse appeared on the scene. He nudged the England captain in the back and said, 'What's the chance of a game tomorrow, captain?' The captain looked at him in complete disbelief. But the horse persisted and said, 'What is the chance of a game tomorrow, skipper?' 'Neigh', said the skipper quickly. 'I didn't ask you to be funny', said the horse, 'I want a game of cricket. I believe that I am the best player in England at the moment.' Just at that moment the batsman slipped and fell on one of those nasty pegs that you have around the nets, damaging himself enough to be carried off. As the horse was there and being persistent he was told to put his pads on. He played the most fantastic shots that you have ever seen. He hit the English fast bowlers all over that nursery ground – whatever they did, he had an answer for. In the end he came out sweating as horses do and said to the skipper, 'Well, am I in?' Well, with one man injured the skipper had no alternative but to play him. The following day England won the toss and in front of 30,000 people, A. Horse went out to bat. A. Horse had won the toss and decided to face the first ball. The bowler was probably the second quickest bowler in the world and he sent the first one down really as a warmer. It swung just a little bit and Horse, with all the elegance of Hammond, hit it to the Tavern fence for four. This upset the bowler just a bit, so he bowled just that little bit quicker and that little bit shorter the next ball. Horse, with the same beautiful elegance, on the up this time, hit the ball first bounce to the Tavern rail. The crowd was quite ecstatic. The third ball of the over was quicker and much shorter. Horse went back on his hind legs and lifted it gently right on to the grandstand roof. As you can imagine, the crowd were cheering like mad. The fourth ball, also short, went in the same direction. By now Horse had faced four balls and had scored 20. The fifth ball was another bouncer but this time outside the off-stump. So, going right up on his hooves he played a beautiful square cut which pitched straight in front of gulley, and before he could move was hitting the boundary rails. The last ball of the over, when the bowler had tried to bowl a yorker, Horse went for a big straight drive, got a thick edge and it went down to third man. Horse was called for a run but didn't move. His

opening partner was two-thirds of the way down the track and the fielder, moving very quickly, threw the ball to the bowler's end and ran him out, he by now prostrate on the ground, having dived to try and get back in. Having picked himself up and dusted himself down, as he passed Horse on the way to the pavilion, between clenched teeth said, 'Why the bleeding hell didn't you run?' 'Run', replied the horse, 'if I could run, mate, I wouldn't be here, I'd be at Epsom.'

Many years ago, when England made their first tour which was to America, the England side visited Niagara Falls. The guide there was delighted to be telling English people all about America. He said, 'Just look at that – Niagara Falls, one of the wonders of the world. Do you realise that there are something like 60,000 gallons of water per second pouring over the top?' Billy Bates, a Yorkshireman, said, 'So there should be, there's nowt to stop it.'

If you took a touring team to Japan every ball you would send down would be a bumper because the Japanese are not very tall. They have one great gift and I have met her. She shares a bath with you and walks up and down on your spine in high heels – the higher the better.

David Sheppard, now Bishop of Liverpool, is well known for his tour of Australia, where his fielding at times was just short of pathetic. One day he returned to the dressing-room after having another bad day in the field, put his head in his hands and dropped it. I often thought that had he put his hands together during the week as he did on Sundays he would have had more success.

The place I, personally, would like to take a cricket tour would be to Tristan da Cunha. It's a volcanic island. There are only 11 people on it, three of those are women, so you would have a very good chance of winning. The type of tour side I would take would consist of drunks, purely and simply because if you go to these volcanic islands it's dust in your mouth all day long, so you have got to have a drink and you've got to have experienced drinkers. Now there was one man, I won't mention his name, Fred Rumsey, who once held up a ship launching for three hours because he wouldn't let go of the bottle. He is the type of man I would like to take with me. My opening bat would be Colin Milburn, because Colin can put a few away. After he has had three or four pints, he goes on to the spirits and the wine. He can take it because he is a big lad, but if you are with him, particularly if you are a woman, you get the glad eye – which is the only one he's got. I wouldn't like all the team to drink. I think that one of them should be a complete teetotaller because someone has to pour. Also on the medical side we would have a masseur. Now nobody really wants a man to do the massage, it has definitely got to be a woman. There is no fun if a man starts to massage you but there is if it's a woman. Mind you, it could mean less runs, but it's worth it. No money would be paid to the players. Each one gets a masseuse of his own and in the middle of the season they can interchange. Colin Milburn would have to have two, one for each cheek.

The sort of manager I would like to have on my tour is someone like Don Revie, who disguises himself and goes off to the Middle East. Quite seriously, you would need a very strong-willed manager to say things like, 'You are next in. I have waited an hour. Can't she leave you alone?' and, 'Will you go in now please?' If we travel to somewhere like Tristan da Cunha, to get the boys really fit I think we should all swim. It's a long way so we would have to start with a large team. By large I mean in numbers, because if we do meet sharks, it's very, very difficult to score runs with one-legged openers – if you will pardon the expression. To attend all the official functions and to go to see the governors, everything like that, you need someone who is erudite, who can talk well, who never slurs his words, or fluffs his lines. The ideal man for this position is, of course, Charlie Chester. Obviously, on tour the best places to stay are hotels. If Ernie was with me then he and I would stay in digs because we are used to digs. A hotel is better because if you want hot water you can always go down to the restaurant and order yourself some soup.

TRISTAN DA CUNHA

Hotels on tour are usually the best hotels available and are very comfortable. In the hot countries they are nearly always air conditioned so the heat doesn't really matter. It is really millionaire style of living, good food, good beds, nice rooms and at all times plenty of hospitality, that's if you want that kind of thing. I have no grumbles about hotels abroad. It was on very odd occasions, too few to mention, that we came across a bad one.

I have been told that when abroad cricketers must at all times realise that they are out there representing their country. Forget about the diplomatic side – you get no diplomatic immunity in any way, you still have to pay all your taxes and act like an Englishman. Players must be capable of being able to hold conversations – in fact it's good training for the future. The social side of cricket is definitely a professional job. An attempt should be made to create a good impression, an impression that should be backed up by feats on the field. There are many things in the social life, at cocktail parties and dinners, which players come to expect. They have to take snide remarks about being English, especially in Australia. Official receptions abroad always used to bore me. It used to be the same old thing. 'We are delighted you are here, we are pleased to see you', knowing full well that at the back of their minds they hope to hell that you are going to get thrashed out of sight on the cricket field. We would have to shake hands, try and be nice to people who made remarks that were sometimes derogatory, but we tried to just pass them over. This was being English and accepting it. This is where I sometimes fell down, when the officials used to think they could say anything they liked to me, but being the person I am, I told them what I thought of them and suddenly I would find myself in trouble. A great number of these people were not really interested in the game. Fifty per cent of them, at least, used to come for curiosity's sake to see what you were like, to see what you looked like, even to see how you were dressed. In my case I always made sure that I was smartly dressed for any occasion and very proudly wore my MCC player's tie. They were there with their crooked fingers, drinking their coffee or their wine, looking down their noses or speaking in some sort of haughty voice that didn't always go down very well with me. It's the same the world over. It has been for a hundred years and I suppose it will be for the next hundred years – officials talking about the game of cricket, thinking they know it all, telling people what to do, especially telling players. It riled me, it did, it really riled me when I was younger. Of course as I've grown older I have learned to accept these things – I suppose that is maturity.

Peter Parfitt Remembers:

When we went to Australia it was always emphasised to you by the establishment at Lord's, how important it was to fly the flag and indeed your MCC colours. It is at important official functions that you always wear your MCC tie. Of course this we did to the best of our ability, but sometimes it did get a little **tiresome**. *People in Australia can be a little boring* **one** *way or another and the sort of thing we got on arrival was, 'What do you think of the sunshine here fellers?', and we would reply, 'Wonderful, it doesn't shine our side at all'. 'What do you think of the beer here fellers?' and we would say, 'Tremendous. You know, we don't have beer in England'. 'What do you think of the Sheila's fellers?' they would say. 'Oh! tremendous, lovely girls, far prettier than those we have in England.' One day a very loud mouthed New South Wales man slapped Fred on the back and said, 'You old son of a bastard, all the way from the home country, what do you think of our bridge?' and Fred said, 'It's not your bloody bridge, it's ours and what's more you haven't bloody well paid for it.' This was absolutely true because when we went back to the hotel very perplexed about the whole affair we took time to check and found that the Sydney Bridge had been built in 1931-32 by Norman Long of Middlesbrough, a Yorkshire firm, and the reason there is a toll charge on the bridge is because it has never ever been paid for.*

Another touring place I would go to, because they supply you with a masseuse, is Sweden. You see the beauty of Sweden is that it has a lot of snow and it's very mountainous and when the fast bowler starts his run up, he lets the ball go early, a long time before he reaches the wicket. By the time it gets to the batsman it is probably 34 feet wide. It is then so big he cannot help but score a lot of runs.

Crowds play a very important part in the game of cricket when you are abroad. They are bound to be behind the home side, this is only to be expected. The most fanatical crowds I think I have ever played in front of are in the West Indies. But I will give the West Indian crowd one thing – they appreciate good cricket, whether it is from their own side or from the touring side. They go to watch two sides battle which I'm afraid a lot of crowds don't. It used to make you feel good to know that anything you were doing, anything outstanding at least, the crowd would appreciate. It makes a big difference to a player when he knows that he is in front of a crowd which actually understands the game and what players on both sides are trying to achieve. Of course, cricket is the West Indian's national game and I wish more crowds in the world would be like them. The remarks they used to shout were funny, witty and very appropriate for that moment but were nearly always in good fun. I know that I had a great time when I was out there.

When going on tour today the modern player wants to jump into an aeroplane and get to his destination within 48 hours. I can't understand them. After a strenuous season I don't think there is anything nicer than being able to relax at sea. Just think, sixteen days in a boat away from the everyday grind of county cricket, enjoying yourself, relaxing, getting over the little aches and pains, taking the sun and getting the sheets of autographs signed ready for the tour. I don't think there is any better way of travelling to, say, Australia or the West Indies, than by boat – complete relaxation. It is a complete holiday, relaxing the mind, relaxing the muscles. You can always tone up in the nets for at least ten days before the first match if the tour is organised correctly. For me, there is nothing like a wonderful trip on a boat across the ocean. It is living like a millionaire without being one.

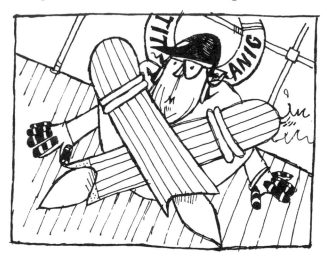

A lot of cricketers don't like flying, well not without a plane. I remember a particular cricketer whose name I have forgotten who wouldn't fly anywhere, that was his thing, he hated aeroplanes. There was a game going on in Ireland before the war and he was supposed to be playing but he wouldn't go over by plane like the rest of the team. He went over by boat. This was in 1939. War was declared while he was crossing and the plane was shot down. It crashed into his boat which sank without trace.

Peter Parfitt Remembers:

Of course the number of stories about Fred are legendary. One I like was after the final Gents and Players match when we were selected to go on tour to Australia. In those days we sailed. Now I suppose we had been out of port about ten days when going down to the blunt end each evening for our social activities, Barry Knight discovered Gordon Pirie on board. Edward Dexter, once again, with his infinite wisdom decided that the one thing we ought to do was to get up each morning at about seven o'clock and tramp around the outside of the decks of the Canberra to keep ourselves fit. I don't think it had ever entered old Edward's mind that the sole purpose of being on board ship for three weeks was to have some rest after an arduous English cricket season. Anyway, we got tramping round the outside of the ship. Of course the one person who flatly refused to do anything at all was F. S. Trueman and he used to sit up at the sharp end of the ship in a deck chair with a huge panama hat on watching us come round every twenty minutes! Gordon Pirie stuck this for about five days and in the end he couldn't stick it any longer and this particular morning he turned to Fred and said, 'Come along, Fred, why don't you join in, it will do you the world of good, it will build your legs up.' I thought Fred was going to have a coronary on the spot, but he replied to Mr Pirie, 'Build my bleeding legs up, I'll tell thee lad, these legs have been going for fourteen years and not let me down yet which is more than your bastards can say for you.'

If the English cricket team goes to India, they must travel first class because they feed them there. They don't feed passengers in the second class, they give them a bowl and allow them to beg in the first. On second thoughts there is no need to travel to India to play that country, you just have to play Bradford.

Travelling in the different countries abroad is pretty easy, you always seem to travel from one state to another by aeroplane. You are picked up by car, driven to the airport, fly to the next airport, get picked up by car and taken to the hotel. Every morning cars or coaches are arranged to take you to the ground, so travel in foreign countries on cricket tours is pretty easy and very well organised. It isn't arduous or strenuous either because usually a match will finish on Tuesday, you fly on the Wednesday, travel to the next venue and have a good night's sleep. As a state match will probably start on the Friday, you then have all Thursday to practice and get over whatever travelling you have done. This is unlike cricket in England where matches finish on the Tuesday night and the touring side then gets into a coach or a train, travels that evening and starts playing again the next day. It is one of the things that is very much wrong with our county system. We play much too much county cricket in Britain for the amount of travelling that has to be done.

TO BED, TO BED; THERE'S KNOCKING AT THE GATE. COME, COME, COME, COME, GIVE ME YOUR HAND. WHAT'S DONE CANNOT BE UNDONE. TO BED, TO BED, TO BED

We have just had a request on the phone from someone reading this book to go out to Greenland to play, because they supply the oil for the masseuses there. They get it from the whale's blubber – so Colin will bo happy. The fast bowlers, if they are playing in Greenland, have got to watch out for the holes in the ice. I mean, it's a nasty thing if you happen to fall down your own ice-hole. In Greenland the days are actually 20 hours long. You start playing around 11 a.m. and at 6.30 p.m. when you would normally finish you have to put on dark glasses to make it look like evening. When you play in Greenland, or Sweden, or anywhere there is snow you don't wear whites, you wear blacks, if they don't mind. I mean some of my best friends are black.

In my early days when I first toured the West Indies, Tony Lock was my room-mate. Tony was a great character. He used to walk about in his sleep. I remember watching him one night, and this is a perfectly true story. He got out of bed, walked across the room to a chest of drawers, opened the top one, stood there for a few minutes, shut it, went to the sink, washed his hands and got back into bed. I thought, that's a peculiar sort of thing to do is that. He seemed to settle down and I must have fallen asleep. When I got up the next morning, I found he had peed in the top drawer and it had run straight through the other four and wet every bloody shirt, underpant, vest and sock we had!

They tell me that Dougie Padgett sleep-walks. He does it regularly and Ray Illingworth, who roomed with him, rescued him on more than one occasion from falling straight down the hotel stairs. There are other room-mates who have no bother about sleep-walking because the condition they go to bed in is such that they couldn't walk when they were awake. The ideal room-mate you could wish to have is the one you never see, and believe me, that does sometimes happen.

You can play cricket in Uganda but it's not the most popular game. The most popular game there is pot black.

Some Final Thoughts

Two things in cricket have always annoyed me — the importance placed on averages, and the unnecessary information the scoreboard provides. I think the printing and publishing of averages should stop and the team selection by averages should stop. Some cricketers play for averages and do so because it is known that selectors and committee members read them when making decisions. I know some committee men who actually take the averages of different players into a committee meeting before picking a side. Very few selectors see all matches. How can performance be compared with averages? I would have all scoreboards showing only the score, the wickets that have fallen, and the overs bowled. I would definitely do away with the actual individual player's score. So many players get into the forties and start playing for their fifty. They tend to go slow to make sure that they get their half century. More often this happens when the player gets into the nineties and there he can be stuck for as long as half an hour, trying to reach his hundred. I think it is both bad for the player and the spectator alike. It would be better if the scoreboard only showed the individual scores to let the crowds know after the batsman is out, or after he has reached his half or full century. Mark you, there are players who count well enough and know exactly how many runs they have scored. A lot can count to five on a good wicket.

The greatest moments of my life are very easy to explain. The first time I pulled on a shirt for Yorkshire, and the first time I pulled on a sweater for England. They were quite easily the most important. Then there was the three hundredth Test wicket, but the practical thing of making a record was not as important as knowing that I was gifted with an ability to play cricket. As I have said, I wish I could turn the clock back 25 years and start all over again. Cricket for me is the greatest game that has ever been invented. A game made for people to enjoy.

Freddie's greatest moment was when he was born. I knew his father, who said to me, 'Eric, it's a boy, so we are going to call him Fred, but he only weighs 3½lb.' 'Keep him anyway', I said, 'he's better than nothing.'

The feeling, when you are taking wickets and you know it's your day and everything is going right for you, is one of the greatest feelings in the world, and could only really be explained by poets and writers. The hard test comes when things are not going your way and you have to grit your teeth,

get your head down and keep going just as if you were taking wickets. There is nothing like taking wickets for any bowler to make him feel more confident, to get his tail up, it's a great feeling. You want to keep bowling for ever. It's on those days when things aren't going right for you that you don't want to bowl and you have to keep telling yourself while everything is hurting that another day everything will be alright. One day you have taken 7 for 20 — walking on air. The next day you have 1 for 100 and your feet are firmly placed back on the ground. I never did like being taken off if I was bowling well and things were starting to go my way. Sometimes I would argue with my captain, but he would usually know if it was my day or not.

I have a love for cricket, and it's a strange thing really because I never played cricket at school. I played football at school, but never played cricket. I never liked cricket until this last ten years. Now I love the game and I have found out why — it's because I love England.

I have enjoyed the opportunity of airing my thoughts in this book, particularly with Eric, Willie and Fred to back me up. Please don't believe everything you hear or read about me — just believe almost everything.

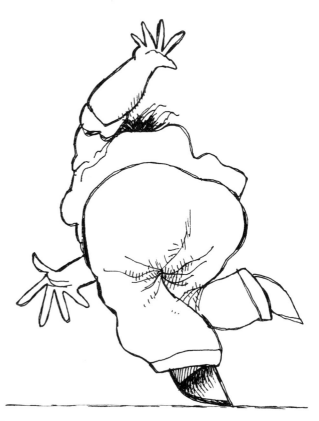

Index